BORN OLD

DAVID WILKERSON

with PHYLLIS MURPHY

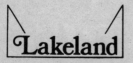

*My parish is the gutter,
and you won't find
any children living in it.
There are only people,
big ones and little ones.
The little people are
born to the big people,
conceived in hate
and shame and sin.
They are born old....*

BORN OLD

LAKELAND
BLUNDELL HOUSE
GOODWOOD ROAD
LONDON S.E.14

© Fleming H. Revell Company 1966
Published in u.s.a. under *The Little People*

First Lakeland edition January 1968
Second impression April 1968
Third impression July 1968
Fourth impression January 1969
Fifth impression November 1969
Sixth impression July 1970
Seventh impression February 1971

isbn 0 551 00015 5

Made and Printed in Great Britain by C. Tinling & Co. Ltd,
London and Prescot.

Preface

My parish is the gutter, and you won't find any children living in it. There are only people, big ones and little ones. The big people are the addicts, the muggers, the prostitutes, the liars, the drug pushers, the burglars, the alcoholics, the con artists—none of them very old in years, but terribly old in misery.

The little people are born to the big people, and the word *children* doesn't belong to them. These are not creatures conceived in hope, love, and obedience to God's will. They are not nourished and warmed and strengthened while their young bodies are forming. You will not hear a good lusty "Here I am!" cry from them when they take their first breath of air, and you won't feel like a mountain of a man when one of them grasps your big finger with all of his incredibly small ones.

The little people are born old. There is hardly anything new about them. They are conceived in the hates and shames and sins of their parents. The body that should harbor them becomes an enemy that feeds them drugs, disease, alcohol. These little people cry when they are born, but not with any hope of being heard and helped. They come into the world with a snarl because they are born wishing they were dead. Let them hold your finger in theirs, and how do you feel? Helpless—and angry, too, because you feel so helpless.

Do these little people—these children without a childhood—belong to anyone? Do they belong to their parents, who sometimes can't remember where they left their babies, who spend every nickel on fifths of liquor instead of quarts of milk? Do they belong to the streets, where the jungle life is often better than the life at home? Do they belong to the institutions, where at least they can be fed, clothed, schooled, kept off the streets and out of our way?

Don't these little people really belong to God? And don't they belong in our way? Are they really part of another world, or have we just shoved them out of ours?

Remember what used to happen in the crowds that followed Jesus everywhere He went? People used to push and shove each other, trying to get close to Him, and the children didn't stand a chance. But Jesus understood that those children needed Him even more than anyone else, and He said, "Let the little children come to me."

He's saying the same thing to us today, only in my parish His words are just a bit different. He says, "Let the little *people* come to me." He understands how things are here.

David Wilkerson

BORN OLD

Jennie was a loner, even in death. In all her life she asked nothing and gave the same. She wouldn't have expected much of a funeral, and the one she got wouldn't have taken her by surprise. It was the cheapest money could buy.

Not that Jennie's family didn't try to do better by her. Carmen, her niece, would have liked something more expensive, but as it was, she didn't know where she was going to find one hundred and ninety dollars, the lowest price she could get.

Carmen was on pretty friendly terms with her neighbors, and they had always felt sorry for Jennie, so she got up her courage and began knocking on doors. She raised a few dollars that way, but only a few. Then she thought of the church—once or twice she'd gone to services at the church down the street—and decided it wouldn't hurt to knock on that door, too. She got ten dollars there; all told, she had fifty. It wasn't nearly enough.

That's how I learned that Jennie was dead. Carmen remembered that Jennie sometimes went to a place called Teen Challenge, and she called me to ask for a contribution. She was very suspicious when I offered her the rest of the money she needed, but she wasn't in a position to turn me down.

"I don't know," she said, and I could sense her desire to hang up the receiver. "I don't know you, mister."

"You don't have to know me. You know Teen Challenge, don't you?"

"No. Titi knows—I don't."

"Who's Titi?"

"Titi is Jennie," she snapped. "Titi means 'Auntie' in Spanish. That's what her family call her—not 'Jennie' like her junkie friends!"

"Listen, you need this money. It doesn't come from me, personally, so you don't have to be afraid to take it." She was silent, but still there. "You can pay it back to us," I said, and that did it. Carmen was a proud woman.

"How soon can I have it?" she asked.

And because she was proud, Carmen must have been embarrassed by the shabbiness of Jennie's funeral. It was held in a small, dingy, bare room—a "chapel," it was called—and the door was wide open to the sounds of other people's grief coming from the adjoining rooms. New business was transacted and old business was stamped "Paid" outside in the hall where we could hear it.

"We" were only a few. Carmen was there with her husband, a quiet, sad-looking man, and so was her mother, who was Jennie's sister. Then there were John Benton, my brother Don, a few of our converts, and I from Teen Challenge, and not a single other mourner.

The casket was closed. Jennie had fallen six stories from the roof of a tenement, and it was better for us to remember her as she had been.

10

Carmen looked a lot like Jennie, but I was surprised when she told me her age. She was twenty-seven, and looked ten years older. Jennie, at thirty-three, had looked ancient, but she was a drug addict. Obviously, Carmen was not; she was "clean." She reminded me of Jennie on one of her good days—there were a few of them; she had the same rounded features in a large rounded face, the warm, dark eyes, and the shining black hair pinned tightly back.

When Carmen turned her head, I saw the thin scar on her right cheek, running from the corner of her mouth, along her jaw, and up to her ear. I had seen that kind of scar many times. It had been made by a razor, and it told me that Carmen's life didn't match the softness in her eyes.

"I'm sorry, Mr. Wilkerson, that I gave you hurt on the telephone," she said, with the stop-and-go lilt that marks the speech of those who must translate their Spanish thoughts into English words. "Gave you hurt" was a thought that didn't translate well, but it made its point quite clearly. "I got to be careful. You know how it is. Titi—Jennie—had those crazy friends." Even as she spoke, she looked back over her shoulder.

"Don't worry," I said. "You won't see them here. Junkies don't have time to go to funerals."

"But I want to see them!" she said, turning from me to John. "They know who did this to Titi, and I got to find out."

Then she saw that we didn't understand. "You thought Jennie jumped off that roof?" she questioned. She guessed the answer, and she was offended by it. Slowly, and with great dignity, she straightened her shoulders. "Jennie Perez did not like to live," she said; "but she did not like to die, either. If you knew her, like you say, you would know that." And I did. "Jennie Perez was pushed off that roof."

"Do you have proof, Carmen?" I asked.

"Yes," she said, but she looked down at the floor. "It was another junkie who did it—I don't know yet which one."

"But why?"

Carmen lifted her head again, and the softness was gone from her eyes. Hate lit them now. "For two dollars! Titi had two dollars on her, and one of her crazy friends found out about it! He saw her going up to that roof—yes, she was going to shoot it up—and he followed her!" Tears muffled Carmen's words, and it was hard for me to understand her. "Titi was so stubborn. She wouldn't give nobody nothin'—he pushed her off!"

"How do you know it was a man?" John remembered to ask.

"I know, that's all." Carmen must have changed her mind then and decided to trust us. "One of the junkies told Titi's daughter. But she's afraid to tell us the man's name."

John didn't hide his surprise any better than I did. "Jennie had a daughter?" I asked.

"You didn't know?" Carmen said. When I shook my head, she took my arm and led me toward the row of folding chairs facing the casket. There was a story she wanted to tell me.

Jennie Perez had three children—as far as Carmen knew, anyway—and the oldest, a girl, was now eighteen. She didn't come to the funeral, Carmen said, because she was ashamed of her mother.

12

"Then Jennie was only fifteen when the girl was born!" I sounded naive, and I felt foolish. I had worked in the slums too long to be shocked by its ways—and yet, I was.

As Carmen talked, I discovered that she had been motivated by something more than a need to trust us. She wanted our help. She had no children of her own, but she had been a mother to Jennie's second child, a six-year-old boy named Pepe. Now that Jennie was dead, Carmen wanted to make an official claim on the boy, and she needed legal advice.

"Well, we aren't lawyers, Carmen, we're ministers." I said. "But we can send you to a good lawyer."

That pleased her. Still, she had something more to ask. She didn't know quite how to say it. "Remember when Titi—Jennie—was 'with the belly'?"

"'With the belly' was another of those phrases that came out in a strange, almost comical, way; it meant "pregnant."

"That was three years ago, the first time she came to Teen Challenge," I said. "What happened after that? Did she have the baby?"

Carmen bent her head. "Yes, a little boy—and he's lost!"

"Lost?"

"She wouldn't let me take care of him!" Carmen said, as if I had blamed her in some way. "She said I wanted him for his welfare money!" She reached for my arm and held on as hard as she could. "Look, Mr. Wilkerson, I don't want money for Jennie's children. I want to give—to give myself, my home. I want to give the care—the heart—." In her excitement, she was mixing up her words, and she stopped, trying to compose her-

13

self. Her husband left his post by the door and came to put his big-knuckled hand on her shoulder.

Carmen had suffered deeply, but it was someone else who touched my heart. *"How can a little baby be lost?"* I asked again.

The answer was simple, as tragedy often is in the crowded, hostile streets of a large city. Jennie couldn't take care of her baby and her habit at the same time, so she "gave" her baby away. It wasn't hard to do. Since Jennie was on relief, she got additional welfare money for the support of her baby; whoever got the baby got the relief money as well. Simple! And horrible, too, because Jennie's baby evidently passed through so many hands that no one could find him now. Carmen had tried.

"I didn't want her to look for him," her husband said. "This is what she got for taking care of Pepe." He turned Carmen's head so that I could see the scar.

"Did Jennie do this?" If she had, then I had been wrong about her. I knew her as hard, but not vicious.

"Her boyfriend," Carmen said, without a hint of bitterness. It was a matter of fact in her life, that's all. "He did this hurt to me because I wouldn't let him take Pepe."

Somewhere, back in my memory something almost forgotten was working its way into the present. It sounded like a cry for help, but the voice was very young and indistinct.

"Can I talk to your lawyer about the baby, too?" Carmen asked, and I nodded. My attention was divided; I was caught up in the question going around and around in my mind.

14

"David?"

I don't know how long I had been standing in the darkened hall outside the rooms where my children slept, or how long Gwen had been watching me. I didn't like to wake her up when I came home late, but I should have known better. Gwen was a sound sleeper, except when our four children or I made the slightest move.

I felt better now that she came to stand beside me. She always knew when something hurt too much to be put into words, and so she didn't ask me what was wrong. She simply talked about the things that were right.

"I understand what you must be thinking," she said, walking with me toward one of the children's bedrooms. "I always feel so good when I see them sleeping peacefully." We went from room to room, checking on each of the small, curled forms, listening to the soft, even breathing. We were sharing one of the most beautiful moments any parents can have—the sight of healthy children, clean and well fed, tired after a day at play in a yard green with summer grass, dressed in freshly laundered pajamas, and sleeping between crisp sheets.

I thanked God for my children. Then I prayed for a child I had never seen, a child who might not even be alive. And if he were alive, what kind of a day was it for him? Where did he sleep this night? Who would hear him, come to him and comfort him, if he cried?

"Gwen—how can a little baby be lost?"

Three times Jennie had slipped through my fingers, and now that she was dead, I became her prisoner. I couldn't get her out of my mind or her child out of my heart.

2

I remembered the last time she had come to the Center; it wasn't different from the first time, except that her performance had improved. Addicts, in general, are very good actors, but Jennie was exceptionally good. She had almost convinced herself that she really wanted to straighten herself out, and I only wish she could have succeeded. But she had come for another reason, and in the end she was loyal to it: she wanted to get clean so that the next time she shot heroin into her veins, it would give her the kick she used to get when she started using drugs.

I didn't blame her for trying to deceive us. There aren't many places where an addict can go to withdraw from drugs, and the Teen Challenge Center has a reputation for offering more than a bed and a meal. We offer love, and with us it is more than a word. Love is the time we spend at a bedside, wiping sweat from a hot forehead; the pacing side by side with a doubled-up kid when the cramps become unbearable; the hand that pulls a warm blanket around shivering shoulders; the reassuring voice that says the worst will soon be over.

17

We aren't special, but our love is, because it comes from God.

"I know your game," Jennie told me the last time she decided to leave. "You're tryin' to get me hooked on Jesus instead of dynamite!"

"Dynamite" is heroin in its purest, most potent form, and while Jennie meant to antagonize me, at least she was comparing Jesus to the most desirable thing she knew. I guess I smiled. "Is that so bad?" I asked.

"Well, it is for me!" She went to the door, but there was something urgent in the way she turned back. "I really dig my old neighborhood—y'unnerstan' what I mean?"

I did. Poor Jennie!

"I can't be like you people here—always servin' God and not doin' nothin' else. Man, I *like* to smoke! I *like* to drink! I like to dance to music with a beat that goes right through me! I can't give it up, not like you people do!" She shook her head impatiently. "No, you wouldn't unnerstan'."

Jennie couldn't wait until something beautiful took the place of the things we asked her to give up. I had to tell her how I felt. "Jennie, if you go this time, you won't be coming back. They'll find your body in a ditch this time."

She laughed and left.

Well, it wasn't a ditch, but a courtyard—a dark, garbage-filled courtyard of a dreary tenement—where they found her body. If only I had been completely wrong!

It didn't need a very bright mind to figure out that Jennie wasn't going to live much longer. For an addict, she was well on in years; and if disease, neglect, and a life of crime didn't take her life, surely another addict would. Junkies aren't generally violent, and they're downright docile when they're high on drugs, but when they need money for a fix, they don't know where to draw the line. No junkie ever means to kill anybody, or even to hurt anybody, but don't count on one to remember anything else when he means to get some money. He'll cheat, rob, and attack his best friend—and that's usually another junkie.

I knew we couldn't hope to reach all God's lost children, but something in me weeps each time we lose someone like Jennie. Now, in losing her, we had lost a baby, too.

I kept trying to imagine how that baby might look, as if I might see him someday on a crowded city street, and I must have walked into the Center like a sleepwalker. In a way, it seemed strange to keep calling it a "Center." That word was perfect for the red brick house where we started, but now we were more like a colony. We owned five of the fine old houses on Clinton Avenue in Brooklyn, and work had begun on a brand new building.

My office was on the second floor of a house that was soon to be torn down to make way for still another new building—ours, too—and I waved absent-mindedly to the staff members who looked out of their offices as I passed. I was going to miss this old house, with its high ceilings and long windows, but I was glad the new building was to have plenty of glass. I like light, and on that bright summer morning my office was full of it. Still, it didn't cheer me.

How wrong I had been last night! It wasn't a new chapter I was discovering, but a very old one. In fact, I had seen it seven years ago.

I had met one of Brooklyn's toughest, most notorious gang leaders, a seventeen-year-old boy named Miguel, who had come to hear me preach in St. Nicholas Arena in New York. That's what kept me busy in those days— I was trying to reach the violent kids of the street gangs to tell them how much God loved them; and those three nights in the Arena told me that the message was getting through. Like most of that rowdy, foul-mouthed, jeering crowd, Miguel had come to heckle, and that's exactly what he did at first. Then, a strange thing happened, and under any other circumstances it would have been embarrassing to him. Miguel became the one who got "bugged," and it was caused by Someone he couldn't see, Someone who reached into his heart and broke it wide open. Miguel began to cry. "Jesus!" he said, and his friends laughed even louder, thinking he was using the word as a curse to offend me. But when Miguel later came to our counseling room and fell to his knees, sobbing and smiling at the same time, his friends became quiet. They, too, could sense another Presence.

Miguel was president of the Hellburners, a gang of boys in Brooklyn's vicious Williamsburg section. When he asked me to talk to his gang about the strange thing that had happened to him, I knew God had sent me a wonderful opportunity.

Miguel wanted me to meet him at his home before I talked to his "boys," and that turned out to be a good idea. I learned what the church was really up against in the city's tenements.

I felt almost foolish when I entered the apartment house where Miguel lived—How could I tell anyone living in such a place that God loved him and cared about him? There it was, bright and early in the morning, and the halls of the building were dark. Someone had taken the light bulb from the only socket. A foul smell almost drove me back to the street. The walls were greasy. Miguel lived on the third floor, and as I went up the stairs, groping my way with each step, I prayed for a special understanding of the things I would see. I could smell the stench of garbage coming up from the alley; there hadn't been a collection for some time.

How could boys like Miguel understand such words as "love" and "care"? And wouldn't the words "eternal life" sound like a cruel joke? By the time I climbed up three flights of stairs, I had learned a lot. Before I told those boys how God felt about them, I had to teach them what those feelings meant.

Miguel seemed to be alone in the apartment—his mother hadn't come home all night—and I waited for him to eat breakfast. "Okay, let's go," he said when he finished his eggs, not even bothering to push his plate back. There it would stay until someone added it to the dirty dishes piled in the cracked, rusty sink.

There seemed to be a lot of rooms in Miguel's apartment, one leading into another, like railroad cars. In fact, it was called a "railroad flat" because the rooms ran from the front to the back of the building. The only windows were in the front and rear rooms; the other rooms were very dim.

As we walked through the apartment toward the front door, I saw beds, most of them unmade and shabby, in every room. There must have been several families living in that one apartment, but that wasn't unusual in Miguel's part of town. A boy like him was lucky if he had a whole cot to himself.

The noise at mealtime and at night must have been maddening, but during the day the rooms were uncomfortably quiet. This wasn't home. It was a place where people came when they had no other place to go. They came exhausted so that they could sleep, in spite of the noise of children crying, parents arguing, doors slamming, feet running on the stairs, radios playing at full volume, fat snapping in a pan. In the morning they got out as fast as they could; it didn't matter where they went, as long as they were gone for a long time.

I had almost overlooked the only occupants who had stayed behind. They were so small, so still, that I walked by them without seeing them. Then I turned back. There on a lumpy sofa in a dingy room sat a little girl and a little boy, following me with their eyes, but not moving a single muscle of their bodies.

"Hello," I said, crouching down. "Who are you?"

They pulled back from me and their eyes narrowed. The little girl lifted her hand to protect her tiny face. I was ashamed. Never in all my life had I frightened a child.

Miguel had come back to me. "C'mon" he said impatiently, not even speaking to the children.

"Who are they, Miguel?"

He laughed. "I guess you could call them my 'brother' and 'sister'—the newest ones."

"But they're scared to death!"

"That's because my mother beats them if they make a move outa this room," he said. He turned away from them, as if the sight of them ashamed him.

"Who takes care of them?"

"You gotta be kidding, preacher! Who's gonna stay in this dump all day?"

They were too young to go to school; the girl was no more than three years old, and the boy was about four. "But what do they do all day? Who feeds them?"

"You got a lot to learn, ain't you!" Miguel said, and he was really losing his patience. "There!" he said, pointing toward the kitchen. I saw a carton of milk and a box of cookies on the windowsill. "They know where the food is! And they keep their mouths shut, that's what they do all day!"

I will never forget those two little faces flushed with hate—for me, for Miguel, for the whole world. There was nothing I could do for them then, but I knew I would probably meet them again someday.

I had an appointment with a gang of boys who had probably spent their childhood just like those little ones, terrified and miserable in an empty room. When they were old enough, they went downstairs to the street, determined to get back at the world. Miguel's brother and sister would grow up to be just like him, maybe worse, and someday I would find myself reaching out to them with the same message I wanted to bring to their brother. Would it ever end?

How many times would I have to pass by on the

other side of the little people, not because I was indifferent to them, but because so many big people were first in line?

I knew, when I left Miguel's apartment, that I had already caught a glimpse of my second ministry in New York. The boy and girl upstairs would not wait for me, but there would be so many others to take their places. Jennie's baby was only one of them.

Memories are time robbers. If Don hadn't looked in on me at lunchtime, I might have spent the whole day gazing out my office window, staring at a busy Brooklyn street and not really seeing it.

3

The Center cafeteria is a few doors away, at 416 Clinton Avenue, the original home of Teen Challenge, and when I wanted peace and quiet I went somewhere else to eat. But that day I had an appetite for noise as well as food, especially the kind of noise I knew I would hear there.

Anyone who expects the Center to be a world of serenity is in for a shock. We don't do anything quietly here, and even our prayers are sometimes good and loud. We take the Bible's advice and "make a joyful noise unto the Lord." Besides, the people who come to us for help are running from a shrill world that screeches after them, and while their nerve ends are worn thin by too many sounds, they would be terrified by a sudden change to silence. We take our people as they come: loud, harsh, and mocking.

At 416 we could count on taunts from the new arrivals, the ones who had come to look us over. They always stayed close to the front door, and spent their time "working angles."

"Welcome, welcome, brothers!" said one of the boys

sarcastically, bowing from the waist in front of us and sweeping off an imaginary hat. The bright yellow sweater he wore didn't belong to him; it was made for a bigger boy and came down almost as far as his knees. I wondered how he could stand it on such a hot day. He was a short boy, and stocky, and he leaped ahead of us, still playing the clown.

"Welcome to the Waldorf! Home of square cheese, square bologna, and square heads!" He got his laugh from the other boys, and he was greedy for more. As he was puffing himself up for an encore, I put my hand on his shoulder and pulled him along with us.

"You're pretty square yourself, son, so you'll be right at home! C'mon!" I said. He resisted, but only for a second. When he saw that I was smiling, not the least bit angry, he shrugged and came along. He was like a chunky Pied Piper for the other boys, who followed us into the cafeteria.

We heard complaints with every mouthful of food, but that was normal. It was good, too. It meant that the boisterous young people who came in off the street felt at ease with us. They weren't afraid to let off a little steam. Don and I worried more about the quiet types, the ones who came in smiling agreeably and saying "yes" to everything. They were harder to reach because they seldom gave us an opening.

On our way back to the office, Don nudged me and nodded toward a boy and an old woman standing on the wide, old-fashioned porch of the office. "That's Jose," he said. "We have an appointment with him."

"Who's the woman?" I asked.

"Must be his grandmother. His mother told me about her. I think she takes care of Jose."

But how? I wondered, as I saw the old woman's swollen, black-stockinged legs. Even while standing still, she was obviously in pain. She wore heavy shoes a few sizes too big, and they looked new, but I doubted that she would ever take enough steps to wear them out.

The boy couldn't stand still. He moved from one end of the porch to the other, checking the path on each side of the house; once he stopped in front of the door and handled the doorknob. He was "casing" the house, mentally working out an escape route, if he should need one. I don't think he was even aware of it. Everything he did was routine, automatic; this was simply his way of entering a strange building.

Jose was all smiles. Jose, in fact, was so much "smiling innocence" that I found it hard to believe he was in serious trouble. He had been expelled from school for disrupting classes, for fighting, for smoking, and for sniffing glue. He was well known to the police as a fighter with a quick temper.

"How old are you, Jose?" I began.

"Eleven, Mr. Wilkerson," he answered, with a note of respect I seldom heard from boys his age. It irritated me because it was overdone, but his grandmother was pleased.

"Why did you make so much trouble for everyone, Jose?" Don asked.

"I didn't do anything, I swear it!" he said. He was small for his age, and he was counting on that to win our sympathy. Well, he had won it, long before he walked into the Center, but he wasn't going to like the way it came out. He sat very straight in his chair, forcing his eyes wide open; he looked defenseless.

"Jose, are you sure you tell the truth?" his grandmother asked.

"Sure, Grandma, don't I always tell the truth? They just don't believe me!" His grandmother wanted to believe him, and Jose sensed it. He went into his act. "Honest, Grandma, you know I wouldn't lie! Not after you taught me not to lie." He threw his arms around her and she cried. "Oh, Grandma, you're the only one who loves me!" he said. For only a second, I saw a contemptuous smile cross his face.

Jose had come to the Center because he thought it would be a better deal than a correction home, to which the court had sentenced him. His mother never wanted much to do with Jose, and usually left him in the care of his grandmother, while she went about her business of having a good time. But now she decided to intervene in his life. She knew what her other son, Jose's older brother, had learned from his cellmate in a reformatory, and she didn't want Jose to turn out the same way. One lying, stealing, no-good hop-head was enough for a family. She had heard about another place for kids in trouble, the place Nicky Cruz was always preaching about, and maybe Jose would be better off there.

Teen Challenge has a good reputation in the courts, and we had legal permission to take care of Jose during a period of probation, if we so agreed—and we were trying to make up our minds about that. When we took in a boy, we wanted to be able to hope he could be saved. Don knew as well as I that Jose needed help; but did Jose know it?

We realized what he was, and he wasn't unique. He was a scheming, deceitful, glue-sniffing, reefer-smoking kid, whose speed and skill with a switchblade knife were deadly. His grandmother thought he was an angel, but her weary old legs kept her from walking down the five flights of stairs to the street, where Jose really lived. She wouldn't have recognized him there. She would have seen those round, innocent eyes narrow as he examined his world for signs of danger.

Jose ran with a gang, not one of the big gangs who used to shake up the city with their rumbles, but a gang of little people, aged eight to twelve. They took their orders from the big people in the big gangs, posing as spies in enemy turf, acting as lookouts on rooftops just before a battle, and carrying the weapons—knives, automobile antennae, bicycle chains, pieces of metal pipe, garbage-can lids, zip guns, ammunition, and sometimes a real gun!

The gangs of big people began to break up a few years ago, as more and more of their members took to drugs. Who wanted to go and fight when he could jab a needle into his arm and forget whatever was bugging him? The big people had no ambition any more, and Jose was more or less out of work.

It wasn't even fun to cut school, because there wasn't anything to do—until Jose met a boy whose mother worked. The boy thought school was for squares, and he threw wild parties in his apartment every day, always making sure that everything was cleaned and put back in place before his mother came home. What a ball! This boy had everything—beer, wine, rock 'n' roll records, girls, marijuana, and glue! You named it, and it was yours! Jose actually felt honored when the boy invited him to join the fun.

I had known so many boys like Jose, and I had known their grandmothers, too. The tired, disappointed women had tried so hard to keep their own children from running wild; now, when they deserved to rest, they had to try all over again with their children's children. No, these women couldn't believe the truth about their Joses. They saw them only for a few minutes every day, usually at mealtimes, but they knew they were good boys. Maybe they did stay out a little late— in fact, the grandmas were usually asleep when their grandchildren crept home at all hours in the morning— but the other boys did the same thing.

I motioned Don to take Jose's grandmother to his office so that I could talk to Jose alone. I couldn't get anywhere with him until I called his bluff, and I didn't want to do it in front of his grandmother. She had been hurt enough.

"All right, Jose," I said, when the door closed, "why do you con your grandmother?"

"You're just like everybody else. You don't believe me when I'm telling the truth!" He was trying me out.

"You wouldn't know the truth if somebody shoved it between your ribs," I said. His eyes narrowed. Now we were getting somewhere. "You were right, Jose. Your grandmother is probably the only human being who loves you. Yet you lie to her." I shook my head when he tried to interrupt. "Don't try your act on me.

I've seen your record. Unless the whole world is lying, you're a real bad character. You're a thief, for one thing. Tell me, Jose, why do you steal?"

"For kicks," he said sullenly.

"I don't buy that. You wanted something more than kicks. What was it? Clothes?"

He glared at me. "I get all the clothes I want from my mother! I don't need anything!" He reached in his pocket and pulled out some grimy, wrinkled bills and held them up proudly. "Y'see this! That's what my old man gives me every week. That's what the court makes him pay!"

"Why didn't your father come with you today, Jose?" I knew what kind of an answer to expect.

"He don't live with us. He and my mother split up a long time ago."

"Do you know where he lives?"

Jose's bluff was almost gone. "No, I only know where he works. I have to go there every Saturday to get my money before he drinks it up." I could imagine how humiliating those Saturday visits must have been.

Of course, Jose was preoccupied with escape routes! His kind of life needs them. Sometimes he just had to get away from the shame of not being wanted by either of his parents. Those were the times when a party at his friend's house wasn't enough to make him forget his anger. He needed something much stronger, and he soon learned where to get it. He didn't even have to go far. Jose's brother lived a few blocks away, and he always kept a few sticks of pot—marijuana—hidden under his mattress. His brother would have beaten him brutally for stealing his reefers, but usually he was busy worrying about his next shot and didn't notice what Jose was doing.

And so they began, Jose's short trips to anywhere in the world. After a few sucking drags on a reefer, Jose became one of the big people, a guy everybody feared. "It was great," he said. "If I wanted to be in Florida, I thought of Florida when I took a drag. Then, man!—there I was on a beach, with the sun shining all warm, and lots of girls in bathing suits!"

I knew what my father would have done if I had had such fantasies—even without the aid of marijuana—at Jose's age. But my father had cared about me, and there wasn't anyone to feel that way about Jose.

"What about the glue?" I asked. "Didn't it make you sick?" I had seen boys nauseous, weak, and gasping for air after trying to sniff glue.

"Only the first few times," Jose explained. "Then your lungs get used to it, and you get a real nice high. Man, I went to Mars one time!" Jose smiled. These were his happy memories, and the probability that he had ruined his lungs to get them meant nothing to him. What was health to Jose? Something that stretched his life out, that's all, and what was life but hell?

Teen Challenge had a new problem to face. It was sitting right in my office, slouched in a chair, dreaming of the day he could leave us and inhale his way into oblivion. Miguel's little brother and sister would be almost Jose's age by now, and probably exactly like him. So would a lot of other children born to the big people we hadn't been able to reach. A whole new generation of rebellion was beginning to make its way in the world, and its future was ugly.

32

I voted in favor of admitting Jose to the Center. The approval had to be unanimous, but I knew Don was already on Jose's side; he had worked with me for nearly four years, and his back was up against the same wall. Maybe we could ask Carlos to keep an eye on Jose; Carlos would be patient with him. He would remember how painful anger could be when it got locked inside a person.

For a long time I had known that my first ministry would never really end. The world will always have teen-agers, and some of them will not know God. But I knew that my second ministry was catching up with me. I had to get to the other Joses before they all became as hardened as the one I had just seen. I had to get to them when they were barely out of the crib.

"Want to make the rounds with me, Dave?" John Benton and Don called from the hall outside my office. I think they felt sorry for me; they knew how I hated to face up to my correspondence. Usually I could count on help from some of our staff, but I had been away speaking at rallies for a few weeks, and the letters were piled high.

4

"You know it!" I said, grateful for a reason to run out on a distasteful job. Actually, the reason was a good one. I needed to get back to the streets, where my ministry began. Speaking at rallies and trying to reach "goodnik" young people interfered with my perspective. Out in the street, in tenement country, Satan ruled the turf, and we had to fight a bloody battle over each soul we tried to rescue.

Our street evangelism had changed since I first preached on a corner in a Brooklyn slum. I got plenty of competition from the brutal energy of the street gangs, always so ready to erupt. My background noises came from screeching tires, police sirens, moans, curses, and screams. My audience was loud, and their language was foul.

I can't say the streets are quiet these days, but the background noises are different, even more frightening. The narcotics trade has changed them.

Addicts don't usually ride around in automobiles. They steal them, break into them, strip them of tires, batteries, radios, and anything they can pull loose in a few furtive seconds, but they don't go joy-riding. There isn't any profit in it.

The police still ride in cars, although they don't use their sirens as often as they did. They try to be quiet in order to catch an addict in the act of committing a crime. That way, they have a reason to pull him into jail. The average addict has a $50-a-day habit; to support it, he has to steal over $200 worth of merchandise each day—$75,000 worth per year—allowing for the loss he has to take in selling stolen goods. I can't blame the city for trying to get the addicts off the street. It's cheaper that way.

Our audience isn't the same any more. They don't say much, and our street workers often preach to people they can barely see. Addicts don't like to come into the light, where they can be spotted by the police, and we have to reach them in their darkened shelters. Sometimes we go into the shadows after them.

Street work is never easy. It's one thing to see a drunk and say a prayer for him; it's something else to walk up to him and tell him right to his face that God loves him and can change his life.

Our street workers knew how it was. So did John Benton. He had been answered with curses and threats; once a woman spat at him. When John joined our staff last year, he didn't know how to tell a junkie from an alcoholic or a person with a mind destroyed by disease, abuse, and depravity. He used to stand on a corner and wonder what he could say to the forgotten, miserable people he saw. How could he approach them? "I began to think I was in the wrong business," he once told me, with that characteristic touch of humor that sometimes covered up the depth of his feelings.

Then, one night, John realized that he didn't have to worry about the words; God would give them to him. John had only to open his mouth. So he walked up to a man stumbling along the street and said, "Hello. I'm a minister. I'm with Teen Challenge. Ever heard of it?" God's way was so much simpler than his, John discovered. It always is.

We were making the rounds of the "needle parks," the streets where addicts dare to congregate in the open. The police can't take them all into jail—there are too many of them, and most of them can't be accused of anything more than loitering—but they keep their eyes on them. The police watch us closely, too. They don't want us to mingle with the junkies because they think we stir them up, and to the police that means trouble. "They're just a bunch of animals," a cop on a beat told us. "They ought to be kept in cages, only we don't have enough cages!"

"I don't think Christ would agree with you," John said, and in such an agreeable way that the policeman lost his patience.

"What would Christ be doing on a street like this?" he shouted, slapping his hand to his head. He walked back to his car, got in, and slammed the door.

This man had asked a question we were trying to answer. Christ had plenty of reason to be in the slums;

and you could find Him there more often than at some better address.

We began our rounds at Fourth Street and Atlantic Avenue in Brooklyn and worked our way into Manhattan, starting in Greenwich Village and going on uptown to Forty-eighth Street, Seventy-second Street, and Ninety-sixth Street. The areas had a lot in common. Except for the spot in the Village, they were on wide streets, heavily trafficked, and lighted by shop windows, movie houses, and neon signs as well as street lamps. During the day these areas belonged to the shoppers, to the people who went home at night. After the sun went down, these streets became the property of the prostitutes, the muggers, the purse snatchers, the pushers, and the addicts, who came out to devour what was left of each other.

Wherever we went, we met friends. They weren't the kind of friends we could count on; they lied to us, led us on, conned us, and would have stolen from us if they thought we carried anything worth a dollar. But, in their way, they trusted us because they knew they could never destroy our friendship for them. Some of them even came out into the light to say "hello."

I couldn't be sure whether it was my imagination, or whether my eyes had been opened, but there seemed to be a lot of children on the streets that night, many more than usual. It was too late for five- and six-year-olds to be up, but there they were, running noisily up and down the dirty passageways between some of the buildings. I didn't see many boys and girls of Jose's age. Would I find them, I wondered, if I went behind some of the buildings? Were they back there in the blackness, crouching under old blankets, choking on the harsh smell of glue, or taking drags on reefers they had stolen from home?

"Hey! John Benton!" A young man ran toward us from the dreary lobby of an old hotel. He was carrying a baby, holding it much too tightly, and I could hear it crying.

"Remember me, Reverend Benton?" he asked when he caught up with us. "I talked to you a couple of months ago." He was panting, and the baby bobbed up and down with his heaving chest.

"Sure, you're Danny!" John said, and introduced him to Don and me. "This is Danny's little girl," he said, pointing to the bundle of dirty blankets in Danny's arms.

"She's sick, Mister Benton, and my wife ain't back yet with the money for the medicine!" Was he trying to con us? The baby was sick; I could see that when I pulled the blanket away from her flushed, swollen face. Her sore, reddened little nose must have been running for hours.

"How old is she?" Don asked.

"Eight months, I think. I have trouble rememberin'." A tiny hand struggled free of the blanket. At eight months, there should have been more flesh on those fragile bones.

"Where's your wife?" I asked, sharply.

"I dunno, honest! She's out gettin' some money—and she better not cop herself a bag, either!" In his coarse junkie jargon, he was telling us that his wife—if she

39

was that—was a prostitute. She was out on the street, "working" to support both their habits.

Danny saw that we weren't taken in. "Look, I need money, all right, but only for the baby! You gotta help her, Mister! He pulled her closer to him, and she cried out.

"Where's the nearest drugstore?" John asked. We both had the same idea.

Danny pointed toward the hotel.

"Here's the deal," I said. "We'll go with you and get the baby's medicine." I could see the relief in his eyes. "*But*—we'll pay the druggist. You don't get to touch the money."

He was angry. "You don't trust me," he growled.

"No, I don't. I never trust a junkie."

"I'm not a junkie! I'm clean! If I wasn't carryin' this kid, I'd show you my arms. They're clean!" the protest was familiar, and I ignored it. Don and I headed for the drugstore, and Danny had no choice but to come along. John waited outside, in case Danny's wife came back.

"Please, pray for me!" Danny whispered, and I saw tears shining on his anxious face. We were standing outside the hotel, still waiting for his wife.

"I gotta kick it this time! Oh, God help me kick it!" he cried. Danny had mustered all his courage and was trying to go without his next fix. He was already experiencing the early physical symptoms of withdrawal.

Don took the baby from Danny's trembling arms. I rested my hand on his shoulder and prayed. "Oh, God, you know how much this boy wants to free himself from his slavery to drugs. He's trying to kick 'cold

40

turkey'; God, and he's trying to do it without help from anybody. Show him that he can't do it alone, God. Show him how much he needs Your Son to help him. Show him that Jesus is right here to help him!"

I tried to convince Danny that he would have a better chance to withdraw if he came back to the Center with us. Maybe his wife would come, too, I suggested. He almost gave in. Then he remembered his daughter. "Can you take care of her while I kick?" he asked.

"Of course, we can," John reassured him.

"We can do better than that," I said. I meant well, but I was about to make a mistake. "We can put her in a good foster home where she'll get love and care." Danny hesitated. Something I said made him suspicious. Then I made another mistake. "Don't worry. She'll still belong to you. We'll have our lawyer draw up some papers—."

"You keep your lousy papers, preacher!" he shouted at me. He seized his baby from Don and backed away. "You won't get me to give up this kid! No papers!"

"But they'll protect your right to your little girl," I explained. It didn't help.

"You want to con me into givin' up my kid! Forget it, Mister!" He turned and ran down the street; and long after I couldn't see him, I heard the sound of his baby's cries.

Later that night, while we were walking along Forty-eighth Street, I learned where I had made my mistake. We heard someone running up behind us, his feet slapping down hard on the pavement with a peculiar sound. We turned and saw a small boy, not more than six or seven years old. He came to a stop and, grabbing our sleeves, puffed out a few pleading words. "Gimme a dime! Gimme a dime!" His wrinkled shirt and short pants were torn, and threads from his worn collar clung to his damp neck. The strange slapping sound of his footsteps came from one of his shoes; the sole was loose and it flapped when he lifted his foot.

We were so stunned by the sight of the boy that we stared at him, wondering what could have terrified him. He was almost hysterical. "Please! Gimme a dime! Oh, gimme a dime!" he screamed.

I thought he was going to pull the sleeve out of my jacket. We all reached into our pockets. I wanted to give this boy everything I had. I found only a few coins in one pocket, and I held them out while I dug into my other pockets. The boy snatched them.

"Thank you! You save my life, mister!" he said, and held out his empty hand to receive more change from Don and John.

"Don't give him any more," I heard someone say. For the moment I had forgotten that there was anyone else in the world except this bright-eyed, frightened child. A girl was standing near us, a tall girl with long brown hair. She was carelessly, rather than poorly, dressed; her clothes were expensive, but wrinkled and stained.

"He's a gypsy boy," she said, "and he's putting on an act."

The boy snorted at her in disgust. "Hop-head!" he said. At his age, he could spot one!

"Here, Gino," the girl said, giving him a dime. "That's all you need tonight. You can go home now."

42

The boy grabbed the coin and ran, his loose sole slapping the ground.

"His family sends the children out to beg at night," the girl explained, as if she were taking on a tour. "If they come home without enough money, they get a beating."

"Then it wasn't an act!" I objected. "The boy really was afraid!"

"Oh, he's afraid," she said, with a patient sigh, "but not in the way you think. Gino's too tough to cry like a baby. He just cries for effect, and you have to admit he's effective."

The girl was intelligent, and her habit had not yet eaten away her insight. She taught us a lot that night. Her name was Shirley, and she had quite a history. At twenty-five, she was the common-law wife of a man serving a long prison sentence, and she was the mother of three children. Here was a woman who must have been a teen-ager when our Teen Challenge street work was beginning. She had been one of the kids we hadn't reached.

Where were Shirley's children while she was out on the street? Shriley didn't know about two of them, but the youngest lived with her mother.

"That's not the best place in the world, though," she said, speaking out of the corner of her mouth as she lit a cigarette. "My mother's a wino."

"Then why don't you try to take care of your child?" I asked.

Shirley blew smoke in a straight line past my shoulder. "Mister, my mother's been a wino ever since I can remember. I grew up thinking kisses just naturally smelled like Muscatel. But she's real steady about her drinking, if you know what I mean. She's not like me. She can take care of herself, and she always goes home at night."

Shirley inhaled again and coughed painfully. Later, she told us that the "welfare people" had two of her children. They had "taken" them away from her, she said, because she couldn't care for them, and now they refused to tell her where the children lived.

I couldn't believe that such a thing could happen. Could children really be taken away from their parents without the parents' consent?

"They throw a lot of papers at you," Shirley said, "and they tell you that you can have your baby back as soon as you're clean. But it's all a lie! The papers are part of a trick to make you give up your kid!"

If this was what the street people believed, I could understand why Danny ran away when I mentioned "papers" to him. I wished we had met Shirley earlier in our rounds; we might have saved a baby. But Shirley herself might lead us to three children if only she would let us help her.

"Did you ever want to kick your habit?" I asked.

"Sure," she said. "Who doesn't? But it's not for me. I almost died."

"I know how rough it is, Shirley. I've seen plenty of girls go through it. They made it, too."

She was interested. I wasn't just another "do-gooder" to her now; I had seen how things were. "Yeah?" she questioned. "What do you give them?"

"Give them?"

44

"You know, pills, or something like that—to help them kick! That's what most of the hospitals do!"

"And did the pills help you?" I asked.

"No," she admitted. "They just made me want the needle more than ever."

"We have something better than pills, Shirley. What's the use of getting clean, no matter how you do it, if it doesn't make you stop wanting junk?"

"Amen!" she said, and caught herself. "Excuse me, Reverends. No offense intended!" Her apology, so clumsily offered, was very touching. It reminded me of a little girl who had been carefully taught to make excuses for the slightest error. "Okay, let's have it," she said, getting back into character. "What are you gonna give me if I kick?"

"Shirley, *I* can't give you a thing. Neither can John, or Don, or any other minister. Only Jesus Christ can give you something to help you kick. He'll give you the strength to do it, and then He'll even take away your desire for drugs. Shirley, you'll be a new person, a whole person—clean and strong!"

Shirley had been watching me intently. Now she threw back her head and laughed. It was a brittle, hoarse cackle of a laugh that cut through me. "No thanks, Mister!" she said, when she had caught her breath. "That's a good speech, but it's too far out, even for a junkie! One thing I'll never be is *clean!*"

Nothing I said could convince her that her future did not have to hold the sins of her past. Redemption, to her mind, was something for the squares, not for the Shirleys.

On our way back to the Center, I thought of Jennie

again. She had a laugh very much like Shirley's. In many other ways, too, they were almost identical.

At first I thought that our work that night had gone very badly. But the more I thought about it, the more each event seemed to be a sign, and each sign pointed in the same direction. That was the way I would have to go.

We sat around in my office when we came back to the Center. None of us said a word, but we could feel the Lord leading us toward the first step we were to take. It was an experience some people might find strange, and perhaps frightening; to us it was familiar, reassuring. We knew He would lead us in a new direction, one we wouldn't have dared to take on our own. We could even feel ourselves pulling back just a little, as we always did. But there was no need to be afraid; there would be light, and the way would be unmistakably marked with more signs.

Finally, I broke the silence. "John, how soon can you possibly move your family here to Brooklyn?" What a question! I didn't blame John for the look of surprise on his face. He and his wife and their three children were only beginning to feel "moved in" in their Long Island home.

I didn't expect John's good-natured grin, and I was grateful for it. "Dave, you sure have a direct way of doing things!" he said, and I knew, from these few words, that our first step had almost been taken.

Teen Challenge had to find a place where the little people could stay while the big people were gaining strength in mind, body, and spirit. We had to be ready, not only for the Dannys, the Jennies, and the Shirleys, but for their children as well. This meant that we had to make some changes in our program.

Until now, we had used two of our buildings as dormitories, one for girls and one for boys. But the dormitories had disadvantages. One street fighter has enough trouble getting along in the world; put him in a room full of other street fighters, and ask him to make the best of it, and you're putting too much pressure on him. The girls had even more trouble than the boys; they were less patient, more explosive, more restless.

We have a farm in Pennsylvania where the boys can stay for a few months after they complete the program at the Center. It was working out well. The boys seemed to appreciate getting away from the city, and in spite of their gripes they welcomed the strictness of the farm routine. They never had to wonder what to do with themselves.

For a while, we sent the girls up to a beautiful estate in New York. Then we discovered something quite simple, but important: you can't treat girls in the same way you treat boys. The girls were homesick for the city; they didn't think the country was quiet at all—as one girl said, "Them birds make a racket!"—and they literally wilted in the midst of so much greenery. So the girls now had a dormitory and little else.

We needed something more homelike for our girls, something that would encourage them to stay at the Center long enough to recover from a lifetime of body blows. We needed a home where each girl could have her own room, and could share in the cooking and housekeeping duties. We could limit the number of girls in each "home," so that they would have an opportunity to live as members of a family, an experience many of these girls had never known.

John and Elsie Benton were "naturals" for the "mother" and "father" of our first girls' home. They had the firmness that could win the respect of girls who were, after all, criminals, and the kindness that could eventually win their trust. I was asking a lot of John; yet he said "yes" even before I told him my reasons for asking.

More of the burdens at the Center would now fall on Don's shoulders, and he accepted them before I could ask for his help. This was one more time when I was grateful for another minister in my own family.

There was work for me, too. I had to find out where the little people could live. I had to learn all I could about the city's welfare facilities, and any other agencies—private or government-operated—that opened their doors to children. I had to see what could be done about cutting red tape, in case we were ever in a hurry to find a home for a child like the one I saw in Danny's arms.

That wasn't enough. I had to put more of my time into getting our first girls' home started. I could help out with street work, with counseling, with hammering nails, perhaps, but I also had to be around when I was needed. The staff were too considerate to call me at home and get me out of bed in the middle of the night, yet these were often the busiest hours at the Center.

There was an empty apartment in an old garage on the Center property; perhaps I could sleep there one or

48

two nights during the week. So many on our staff were already living in, and during the next several weeks, even more of a burden would fall on their shoulders. I couldn't ask them to do something I was unwilling to do; I had to give my time, too.

I felt very humble. I had asked a great deal of some people who were already giving all they had. They answered by offering more than I asked. This was one of those signs that marked the way we were to follow.

What is a "family"? What is a "home"? How do you define these words to someone who hasn't really lived them? We weren't sure; nevertheless, we were trying to learn.

5

In three months' time, the Center had created a family. I could sense a change in the atmosphere, and although there were more than the average family's problems and conflicts, I felt that we were making progress toward solving them.

Across the street from the office was an old, gracious, three-story house full of hand-carved chestnut woodwork. It had known better days, days when light-footed young ladies spoke in whispers and closed doors quietly. Now it was "home" for John and Elsie Benton, for their three children, and for their "adopted" temporary family—three street-hardened girls who slammed doors, shouted to each other from one floor to another, and ran up and down the stairs as if they held a personal grudge against each step. The old house was making new history, and I doubt it had ever known more useful days.

Lots of girls had come and gone during the three months since we had opened the door to our girls' home: some of them stayed only a day or two; some of them kept coming back and leaving again. We were

51

becoming used to that. Only three girls had stayed on, and because of them we dared to hope that our brand of family life would work.

Eva came from one of the most violent sections of Harlem, and she had ruled her turf there, until she got hooked on drugs. Then she drifted away from her gang and took to burglary, mugging, and prostitution, in that order; finally she went into business for herself, as a drug pusher, but, as she put it, an addict is too greedy to make a profit out of selling "the stuff." Eva read about us in my book *The Cross and the Switchblade* while she was in jail. When she was released, she came to us, daring us to knock the enormous chip off her shoulder.

Poor Eva! She was a thorny girl and very touchy. Her term in prison had given her an opportunity to regain her health and put on some weight, and she came to us in much better condition than most addicts. She was a loud, big-boned, good-looking girl, obviously strong enough to carry on the terrible threats she made to us. She was particularly sensitive about her color, and read "prejudice" into every word we uttered. I really winced when John and Elsie took charge of her.

Love, patience, and disciplined family life had made some amazing changes in Eva. She was growing up right before our eyes. She no longer laughed during chapel services, and she was trying to pray. At first, she used to listen to the others who were praying; then she would borrow a word here and a word there, and put them together in a way she hoped would sound right. Finally she seemed to realize that prayer is more than words—it is our way of talking to God. He is our Friend, and so we don't have to be very formal when we talk to Him. One day I heard Eva saying, "Listen, Lord, you gotta help get my mind off wanting a cigarette!" She was beginning to understand where she could go for help when the old temptations got to be too much for her.

Eva had two beautiful little girls. I knew they were beautiful because she had shown me a photograph of them. It was a color photograph, faded by time and cracked from being handled.

"Is this the way they look today?" I asked.

"I don't know," she said sadly. "They won't let me have anything to do with them."

"Who won't?"

"My grandparents. They live down South. That's where my kids are—with them."

Here were two little people we probably would never meet, because there was hardly any chance that they would be reunited with their parents. Eva's husband was an alcoholic who saw nothing wrong with his way of life, and Eva herself had far to go toward complete recovery. But I worried about her children as if I knew them well. Who would take care of them if something happened to their grandparents?

Margarita had no children. She was still one of the little people, and how well she knew it! Margarita somehow got the idea that the word "juvenile" gave her the right to commit a crime and get away with it. At fifteen, she was already an addict, a pusher, and a common thief; she may have been more, but she didn't admit to it. "They didn't know what to do with me, 'cause I'm so young," she said, in her sing-song, dreamy way, describing her experiences with the law.

The pattern had changed one day, and Margarita found herself in jail. She was put in "the tank," a large cell where recently arrested people are kept until they are assigned to less crowded quarters. Margarita was surrounded by frightened people, abusive people, sick and moaning people, none of whom had the slightest regard for her tender age.

Margarita was badly shaken. The next day, when a social worker urged her to seek a way to break her habit, she was only too willing to agree. Until then, she hadn't been convinced that she was doing anything wrong; now she still wasn't sure, but she knew that, right or wrong, her habit was leading to trouble.

The social worker mentioned a few places where Margarita might go to kick her habit, provided the judge suspended her sentence and put her on probation. One of the names was familiar; some of the boys Margarita knew used to talk about Teen Challenge. She would go there, if they would take her, and she wasn't sure they would. "Like—who am I? I'm nothin'" I had heard Margarita say; she believed it, too.

"Home" at the Center was very different from the home Margarita had known. She had lived most of her life with her mother and her mother's "old man" (by this she meant her mother's boyfriend, not her father). He was cruel, and he used to beat Margarita until she bled because she refused to call him "daddy." She hated him for that, but she would never forgive her mother for standing by and letting him do it. "I love my mother," she said. "I know you gotta love your mother, no matter what she does, right? Well, I just can't forgive mine, that's all!"

Little people like Margarita don't always want to be rescued. Life on the bottom of the world is too new to them, too much of an adventure. It takes time for them to realize that they are trapped. It takes time for the adventure to turn to horror, for the horror to turn to desperation. Only then do they realize that nothing in the world can help them. Only then do they cry out for a Saviour.

We couldn't be sure whether Margarita would make it. It was too early to tell. But we all agreed about Chickie, the third girl who stayed with us: Chickie seemed hopeless. She was a perfect example of a hold-out. She wanted nothing to do with Jesus Christ, and she did her best to make Him feel the same way about her. Everyone else in Chickie's life had given up on her—why not God, too?

It was true. There wasn't a single person who wished Chickie well. Her grandmother's love, the last to go, died slowly, one tear at a time, as Chickie changed from an obedient, affectionate child into a "deb" whose bloodcurdling screams spurred her gang of girls into brutal street fights.

What had changed Chickie? Was it the shock of a new environment after her family moved from Puerto Rico to New York when Chickie was only thirteen? Was it the family itself? Chickie had no father; her mother, only fourteen years older than Chickie, was still a wild and wayward problem to her worried grandmother. Chickie met a lot of other relatives in the city, people she never knew existed, and they all lived together in a dilapidated apartment. Space was so scarce that one of Chickie's cousins, an infant, slept in a bureau drawer. Was this what changed Chickie? Or was it the schoolyard, where twenty grim, silent girls waited for her at three o'clock on her first day in school? Was it the feeling of achievement, of importance, that came to her when she proved she could take their blows without uttering a sound? Was it the look of fear in the eyes of the girls when Chickie went on to prove that she could return the blows with a savage fury? *All* these things had changed Chickie.

I had a glimpse of the girl she must have been when we interviewed her. She seemed almost shy. But once she was admitted to our program, the joke was on us. Chickie smiled at everything we said and did, and our chapel services made her giggle. She constantly looked for trouble, and she needled the other girls until they cried, or, better yet, tried to fight with her. She could always beat them, and she enjoyed the sight of their tears. Crying was something she boasted she simply could not do.

Chickie, at twenty-four, was already an old-timer in the ways of drugs and crime. But life on the bottom of the world seemed to agree with her, and as far as we could tell, it hadn't yet worn her out. She was a tiny, wiry girl with an enormous amount of energy when she was clean; unfortunately she used all her strength to feed her weakness—junk.

Chickie irritated us, and she was the worst kind of influence on the other girls. She was pushing our system of discipline to its limits, trying to break it down completely. But Chickie had a little boy, and every time I thought we would have to dismiss her, I remembered him. He was living with Chickie's grandmother, an old and tired woman whose heart had been broken far too many times. Someone had to think about the boy's future.

We had to try to stretch our patience where Chickie was concerned. Her baby deserved at least that much of a chance.

Not all the big people came to us by themselves. Sometimes they came in pairs, claiming they were married. We never took their word for it. During the first six weeks they stayed at the Center, all couples lived apart. Then, if they could produce marriage certificates, they were given an apartment in one of our buildings. Otherwise, they stayed apart, or left the Center.

The couples who came to us from the city's poorest, most crowded streets made very poor husbands and wives. These people were handicapped in every conceivable way—mentally, emotionally, physically, and spiritually. They could barely take care of themselves, and any attempt to take on another burden was doomed to fail. Yet they married, and it wasn't so hard to understand why: they were miserable, and, like so many of us, they were desperately lonely.

Marriage didn't help them. Their loneliness continued, and, if anything, their lives were more miserable because they were even more abnormal. Slum husbands don't like to work, even if they can find a job— and they rarely can. A job means responsibility, which is something these men don't want. They've had too much of it, since the day they were born. They've never had a childhood; they had to grow up right away and take the place of the father who was either dead or unknown. But a little boy can't play the little man for very long. Pretty soon he gives up and lets the women take over. He just wants out.

You can find most of these slum husbands loafing in their filthy apartments during the day. Sometimes they go out to stand around with other men in doorways and on corners. They pass the time by swapping stories about the latest ways to get high. Toward nightfall, they get restless; that's when their wives go out to get money. If the women have a profitable night, the men can look forward to staying high most of the next day.

Slum wives get nothing out of marriage, yet they are usually the ones who try to hold the marriages together. The wives bring in the money, in any way they can get it, and the fastest, surest, most accessible way is prostitution. They'd rather make a living by stealing, but that holds too many more risks; the police are harder on thieves.

Companionship is a joke in these marriages. In fact, a husband and wife often go their separate ways most of the day, except for the time they spend checking up on each other. Mutual suspicion is next to the strongest bond they have (the strongest is their habit). A husband wants to be sure his wife isn't holding out some of her money for herself; and a wife keeps her eye on a husband because his habit could easily gobble up the income from more than one woman. There are fights, brutal ones. Sometimes there are deaths.

Anna and Robert fought so violently that it shocked them into reality. It was their habit or their lives, they decided, and so they came to us. They came listlessly, with little hope for a cure. We were simply the last stop on the way to death, and, as they said, what could they lose?

"I know you can't cure an addict," Anna said wistfully, "and we've been on drugs for eight, maybe nine, years."

"Yes, you can be cured, Anna," I said. "I'm not talking about an ordinary kind of cure. We're not going to put a bandage on the part of your life that hurts. That wouldn't do any good. What you need is a whole new being."

"I needed that since I was born," she sighed.

"You can be born all over again," I said, "into a completely new life."

She didn't trust me. She was preparing herself for the punch line of a straight-faced joke. "Yeah, sure. And I suppose I won't have any arms, either, so's I can't put a needle in 'em!" Anna must have dared to hope at some period in her past, and life had beaten her very badly for it. Now, even the memory of hope was painful to her.

"Anna, you won't lose anything but the sin that's held you prisoner all your life. You'll still have your arms, your legs, your eyes—everything you have now. But your sin will be gone, and you'll be new and clean."

"How're you gonna do that?" she asked, but it was an honest question; the bitterness had left her voice.

"*I* can't. You can't, either. It's already been done, by the Son of God, Jesus Christ."

"Then how come I'm not new and clean now?" she asked. I had confused her.

"You will be, Anna, once you believe in Christ's power to make you clean. You see, He already paid the price for the sins you committed." She was even more confused. "Jesus Christ took the rap for you, Anna," I explained. "It's as if you stole something, and the cops came after you. Then, when they caught up with you, Jesus stepped in between you and them, and said, 'Here, take Me instead.' Understand?"

Now she did. Her eyes never left my face.

"Jesus did the same thing for me, Anna, and for everybody else on the face of this earth. But a lot of people still don't believe it. When He was up on that cross, He had nails in His hands and nails in His feet, but that isn't what held Him there. He was bleeding, He was in terrible pain, yet He could have stopped it in a second. He was the Son of God, and He didn't have to let people crucify Him! You see, He *wanted* to stay there, because He had a special reason for being on that cross. It was really meant for us. We were the ones who were supposed to suffer and die for the sins we couldn't help committing. But Jesus stepped in between death and us and said, 'Here, take Me instead.'"

I saw tears in Anna's eyes. "Don't think we didn't deserve to die, Anna. We did, just as you would deserve to be punished for stealing something. Now you know how much Jesus did for you. And He keeps doing it, over and over." A look of puzzlement crossed her face. "No, Anna, He isn't dead. He's alive—here—this very minute. He died on that cross, all right, but God brought Him back to life! That was God's way of saying that you and I don't have to die for our sins, either. Anna, death is a rotten way for life to end. It's an O.D. from the devil. Your life doesn't have to end that way, not if you believe in Jesus Christ. The life He can give to you will never end."

I hadn't intended to say so much at one time, but Anna seemed to be hungry to hear it. I hoped so, because soon Anna would become a mother, and it would be wonderful if she and her baby could begin their lives together.

I hoped, too, that Anna's husband would be ready to begin life with her, but Robert wasn't responding very well to a normal routine of married life. "I gotta do too much!" he complained. "Get up, go here, go there, don't be late for class, sit down, eat, do your homework, pray, go to sleep! You people are always doin' things! Don't you ever goof off?"

Routine was hard on our converts, yet in some ways they welcomed our rules and regulations. They didn't like to make decisions, so we put them on a schedule that told them exactly where to go and what to do each minute of the day. We kept them busy, which was something new and exhausting for them; we also kept them from wondering what to do with themselves, and they appreciated it. Idleness was their deadly foe, and many of them had taken their first puff of marijuana because they couldn't think of anything better to do with their time.

We already had one baby at the Center, and we were trying to hold onto her. Our chances weren't good.

Little Sandra was the four-month-old daughter of

Beverly and Pedro, two of Teen Challenge's most promising converts—until they went out on their own. Something happened to this radiant young couple who waved goodbye to us almost two years earlier. They were leaving to go to Bible school and, hopefully, a future in the missionary field. At first, I received happily scrawled letters full of exciting news; the most important bulletin was the expected birth of their baby. Then the letters stopped coming, and the next news I received was bad. Beverly and Pedro were in jail. They had run off from Bible school, and in their panic they fell back on an older, more familiar way of life—stealing. They were caught and arrested.

I had another lesson to learn about the big people out on the streets. I was beginning to realize that I could never breathe a sigh of relief for any of them who came to us; there was so little left of them by the time they turned to God, and the hands that clutched His mighty one were feeble beyond belief. I used to think that it was only a matter of time until our converts could grow strong enough in their faith to live healthy, useful lives; this was still true, but it was also imcomplete. Our converts couldn't go out on their own simply because they were saved and they believed. The moment they left us, the world barged in between them and God, and they felt confused, frightened, abandoned.

I had looked at our converts in the light for too long. I had seen them happy and smiling; I had watched them helping others like themselves, and thanking God for the strength to do it. I had forgotten how wretched these young men and women had once been, and for how long. We had to keep them close to God for a much longer time, until His way of life became second nature, habitual, to them.

Could a baby like Sandra wait that long? I doubted it. She was born a few months after we bailed her mother and father out of jail, and it was mainly because of her that we offered her parents an apartment at the Center. Beverly and Pedro didn't want to come. They were trying to cover their shame with defiance, and they didn't like to ask us for help. We knew that, and we tried to make it unnecessary for them to ask. We referred them to a capable lawyer, and Don, John Benton, and I went to court on the day their case was heard. Our prayers were answered when the judge suspended sentence and put them on probation. "Praise God!" we shouted, probably astonishing the court officials, and not caring if we did. Beverly offered a prayer of thanks, and we joined her in a chorus of voices that surely only God could comprehend. But Pedro stood apart, silent and frowning; he had no praise to offer. Unlike Beverly, who had fallen away from God, Pedro had actually turned his back on God. That was a big difference.

I didn't think this unhappy family would stay with us for very long. When any of our staff tried to look in on Sandra, her mother and father accused them of spying. It wasn't true. We were aware of their comings and goings, but not because we were curious. No one could blame us for falling in love with a beautiful, blue-eyed, round-faced, gurgly, little girl with a fuzz of light brown hair on her tiny head. She was such a good child, with such a wonderful disposition, that most parents would have made fools of themselves at her crib-side. It was hard for us to understand Beverly and Pedro. At times they seemed to forget Sandra existed, and we knew that they were leaving her alone more times than they admitted. Day by day, we were losing all three of them.

Doris and Felix were the third couple living at the Center that autumn. They were responding only slightly better than Beverly and Pedro, but at that point even a little encouragement could drive me to my knees.

I was surprised that Doris came to the Center. She was one of the hardest, coldest women I've ever met; her eyes peered out at the world as if she held some secret grudge against everyone in it. Yet Doris was the one who decided that she and Felix needed help; and where Doris went, Felix followed. If he didn't, she sometimes beat him up. (The first time I heard of such a thing, I almost sputtered. Then I began to see that it wasn't the least bit uncommon in these "street" marriages, where the roles of husband and wife were often confused.)

An interesting change began to come over Felix after he spent a few days at the Center. Sick as he was from kicking "cold turkey," he insisted on dragging himself to chapel services. Doris stayed in bed, tossing and moaning at any of the staff who tried to comfort her. I think she was furious at Felix for being sick in his own way instead of hers.

The differences between Doris and Felix increased after the physical part of their habit was broken. Felix took a deep interest in his classes and in our entire program. Removed from drugs, he was a compassionate young man with a keen sense of other people's needs.

Doris, however, began to live in her drug-blurred past. She couldn't remember much of it, not after such a long habit, but she never tired of talking about the other times she had withdrawn. She ticked off the dates and the names of the various hospitals on her fingers, as if she were keeping track of some very important world events. None of the cures had "taken," according to her, and she hinted quite proudly that our program was no better than the others. I had the feeling that Doris had changed her mind about giving up drugs, and I wondered how long she would wait to go back to them.

At first, I thought Doris was simply hanging around, waiting for Felix to see things her way. Then, one day, she admitted to me that she was pregnant; this was her real reason for coming to us.

"You really want this baby, don't you, Doris?" I asked. For only a moment, I saw something gentle in her eyes.

"Yes," she said. "And I want to keep this baby! The word got around that you people could help me." Doris and Felix had two other children—boys, seven and nine years old—but they acknowledged their failure as parents. "When I wanted a fix, I couldn't stand my kids," Doris told me. "I'd stay out of the house for hours, so I wouldn't have to hear them cry." She was ashamed of the way she had treated her children; and because she could not live with them and with her conscience at the same time, she gave her boys over to the care of the welfare department.

We couldn't help Doris or her unborn child unless Doris began to respond, and she showed no sign of it. Felix wouldn't be able to help her, either; she was more likely to take him with her when she went back onto the street.

The time I was spending at the Center was little enough. There was enough work to keep me there permanently; but I also needed my own family, just as much as I hoped they needed me.

Counseling with our converts took more time than I expected. I should have realized that we would run into more complications now that we were taking on family-size problems. But out of all the arguments and personality conflicts, a family spirit of patience and tolerance was growing, and that was good.

Jose was often on my conscience. It was hard to believe that this sweet-natured, agreeable boy had once boasted of lying to his grandmother. "She's a Christian," he had told me then, "and she'll believe anything!" Well, Jose was a Christian now, and he knew better. He believed in his Saviour, and out of that faith came some remarkable changes in his life.

Jose had started attending school near the Center, and at first I wasn't sure it was a practical move. The Center is on a fairly pleasant street, but the general neighborhood is rough. Many of Jose's classmates would be trouble-makers, as he had been, and he would be the new boy in class. It was risky.

The first day at school was painful for Jose, and so were the ones that followed. He was needled, pushed, called names, any one of which previously would have brought him out snarling, open knife in hand. Jose, in fact, didn't need a knife; he could have been lethal with a ruler or even an ordinary pencil. Instead, he took the hardest way of all: he ignored everything the other boys did to him. By no means was he ready to offer them friendliness, but he had taken an important step by not wanting to kill them.

Carlos had become a wonderful influence on Jose. He was someone Jose could respect and look up to, and Jose had never known a friend like him.

I wanted to be sure that Jose could have the opportunity to take more steps toward a useful life after he left us. His probation period would end in a few more months, and I hadn't had time to think about where he would live after we no longer had legal custody of him.

If Jose went back to his old neighborhood, to the same courtyards and alleys where his old friends surely were still sniffing glue, he would lose everything he had gained. Even his grandmother didn't want him to come home, much as she missed him. She understood now that he had lived another life down there on the street five floors below her, and she didn't want him to return to it. She was willing to force her tired old legs to travel a great distance in order to see Jose, if only he could live in a decent home.

Jose's grandmother wanted to commit him to the care of the city welfare department, at least temporarily, until she could find a way to move to a better neighborhood. I was inclined to agree with her. One of the welfare homes might be the answer to Jose's problem. He could do a lot worse.

Of the more than seventy institutions offering some sort of haven to New York City children in need of one, ten come under the authority of a city welfare department. These are by far the most crowded foster homes; their doors are never closed in any child's face. Here, all comers are accepted, which is something that can't always be said of the other institutions, both private and religious. The city does not pick and choose on the basis of race, religion, color, sex, or economic background.

Most of the children in the welfare department homes come from the poorest, least educated, most deprived of the city's citizens. Here the minority groups are unhappily in the majority, for here is where they must come when every other helping hand is withdrawn from them. There are those who blame minority groups for their desperate way of life, but here, in these huge institutions serving as "home" for so many Negro and Latin-American children, anyone can see that desperation is the only way of life open to them. Looking at the hundreds of children temporarily or permanently homeless, it is easy to claim that minority groups aren't taking care of their own. This is not true. There are many, many privileged children abandoned by white parents of better means; they are not as conspicuous because there is no shortage of doorsteps on which they may be left.

The children's bureau of the New York City welfare department is authorized to provide *temporary* shelter and care for children who, for one reason or another, cannot be cared for in their own homes. This they most certainly do, but often the word *temporary* must be stretched into a matter of many years because some parents do not come back for their children. It's pretty hard for those who spend most of their young years in one of the city homes. Many of the other children come in one day and go home the next, which is a painful disturbance to those who endlessly wait.

Children are brought to welfare department homes for many reasons. Sometimes a mother must go to a hospital for treatment of an illness, and the father cannot afford to lose a day's pay and stay home to look after his children; sometimes a mother has serious emotional problems and needs a little time away from the demands of caring for her children. In these cases, the children usually spend their days at the welfare homes and return to their families in time for dinner. Some children come to the shelters because a mother is dead and a father needs time to adjust his life to her absence; these children may have to stay a little longer.

Whenever possible, the welfare authorities try to keep a home intact. They will even send "home workers" to cook and clean, and supervise the children for a troubled family, in the hope that this will keep the family members together during their time of distress. Still, the homes keep breaking up, and the children come to live in the city's shelters.

Then there are the handicapped children, the neglected children, the unwed-mothers-to-be "children" under eighteen years of age. The city takes care of them, too, when they have nowhere else to go.

It's the same story in each case, no matter how or why they come: if they could afford private care and treatment, they wouldn't be there. But no one, no matter what price he might pay, could hope to get better care.

I was very surprised when I first became acquainted with people in the welfare department. I had expected efficiency, and a high degree of education, which of course I found; but I also found compassion. These people are highly trained to deal with human anguish in every conceivable form, and they don't handle misery from a distance; they wade right in up to their eyeballs.

Jose would not be a stranger to the staff members of the children's homes. One of the reasons why these institutions are so crowded is that so many children come to them by way of the courts. Some, like Jose, are seriously delinquent and in need of a properly supervised environment; some have been placed under the temporary care of the welfare department because they were cruelly abused in their natural homes. If Jose went to one of the shelters, he would be among people who truly wanted to help him.

I remembered a morning when Don, John, and I went to visit a city home for boys. We had just entered the lobby when a loud bell clanged, signaling a fire drill. I had the same reaction I used to have when I was a little boy in grammar school. "Oh, no!" I groaned.

Within seconds after the alarm sounded, boys of all sizes suddenly hurried into the lobby from every direction. A staff member politely directed us to a hallway off the lobby, where we found ourselves among still more boys, most of them Negroes, from eight to ten years old. They were a touching sight, those orderly, well-scrubbed, neatly dressed, alert youngsters. They were, in fact, so well behaved that I was embarrassed to find that we three were the only people talking.

When I was a schoolboy, I found it almost impossible to stand still and keep quiet during a fire drill, especially after the first minute or two. But the people in charge of the boys' home had found a way of putting the time to good use.

A tall, deep-voiced man clapped his hands for attention. "That's pretty good, boys," he said. "You made it down here in exactly 2 minutes and 40 seconds." There were murmurs of pride. "The last time we had a fire drill, it took you 2 minutes and 58 seconds. Now, how much faster did you move today? How many seconds did you save?"

Several hands shot up, waving frantically. Some of the more competitive boys called out the first numbers that came into their heads. "Ninety-seven!" "Three!" "One hundred and four!"

"No, no, boys, you're just saying words," the tall man said, with a gentle laugh. "You have to use your *heads* to find the answer. Try again."

This time no hands went up. Everyone was silent, and the young faces around me were screwed up in exaggerated expressions of concentration. Then a hand went up, and then two more. Quickly, the tall man pointed to the first volunteer, who called out, "Eighteen seconds!"

"That's *right!*" said the man, with a big grin that included every boy in the hall, as if all of them had come up with the right answer. Then he checked his watch and saw that the drill was ended. In those few moments, the boys had learned that arithmetic wasn't something to be kept in a classroom; they could carry it around with them in their heads, and use it to solve some problems, too. There was a look of happy discovery on the boys' faces as they filed out of the hall and back to their classrooms.

Until I saw them for myself, I thought such large welfare institutions were, by their nature, cold. I was wrong. Of course, Jose would live in a room painted the inevitable "institutional" green, but its monotony would probably be broken up by some cheerful pictures painted by the staff in their free time. The children, too, were welcome to add their pictures to the display, and some of them did, but most of those who began to paint left before they could complete a picture.

The biggest problem in the public-supported children's homes was overcrowding. Jose, for example, would have his own bed, but he would sleep in a room filled with many more beds than it was supposed to accomodate. His bed would have its own supply of linen and a neat bedspread. He would have a closet of his own in a long line of other closets; some of them were built along a wall, while others, more recently erected, intruded into the aisles between the beds. The closets I saw had no doors, but I don't suppose boys care about such things; in fact, they probably appreciate the ease with which they can get at their clothes in the mornings.

Jose already had more than the average wardrobe I had seen. I remembered being shown through some boys' dorms while the occupants were in school, and I noticed that most of the closets held a change of underwear for the next day, a fresh shirt, a handkerchief, socks, and a clean pair of pajamas. A tie hung from a hook; it was seldom used. A towel and a face cloth hung from other hooks. Sometimes there was a pair of shoes on a closet floor, meaning that the owner had a second pair, probably sneakers, which he was wearing at the time. I was impressed by the extraordinary neatness I saw everywhere I looked; there was a place for everything, and everything was exactly in its place—but there were so very few *things!* Too many of the boys obviously owned nothing but the clothes given them by the welfare department, and must have brought nothing with them when they came. Jose, with his few simple changes of clothes, would seem extremely well-to-do by comparison.

I shook my head. In my anxiety about Jose, I had allowed myself to forget something I had learned. I used to be like Jose's grandmother—and like most other people, too; I used to think the government was supposed to handle problems when they became too big for people, and I surely would have classified Jose as one of those problems. But when I began to see how many of our problems were already falling on the shoulders of the government agencies, I felt just a bit ashamed. People do not cease to be human beings when they are in trouble; yet when we begin to think of them as "problems," we sometimes forget that they are our fellow men. They have a claim on us because we are all made in the same image; we have the same Father, and we are only kidding ourselves if we think we can turn our backs on each other.

Rightfully, Jose was Teen Challenge's problem; he was our human being in trouble, and we had no right to drop him in someone else's lap. The welfare agencies had plenty of work, and I'll never know how they did it so well. Now it was time for them to get some help from the rest of us.

The next morning I learned that John's "adopted" family was about to increase. During the night he had had a phone call from Shirley, the young woman we met on our rounds during the summer. Shirley had changed her mind; she wanted to kick her habit.

7

John didn't look happy. "She's got real problems, Dave," he explained. "She's tried to kick before, and she always went into convulsions. That's why she wants medication."

I didn't know what to say. I wondered whether Shirley had told John the truth. It wasn't likely, but if she had, we faced a difficult decision. We insisted that our converts kick their habits the hard way, the only way—"cold turkey," without any medication whatsoever. We have never broken that rule.

I should have realized how much John had learned about addicts in his year with us. He automatically doubted Shirley's story until he checked it against some of her prison and hospital records. Then he began to worry; Shirley was telling the truth about her convulsions.

"I don't know, Dave," John said. "This sounds dangerous to me. Do you think we should send her on to a hospital?"

"Will she go?"

77

Sadly, he shook his head. "No. She wants to come here, and nowhere else."

We were thoughtful. Neither of us wanted to be the first to suggest changing our policy and providing a mild form of medication for Shirley. We realized that even one small change meant the end of the entire policy. One junkie would tell another; the converts who had already gone through cold turkey would feel betrayed.

"Tell you what," I said. "Call our doctor and tell him about Shirley's condition. Ask him what he thinks we ought to do." If John thought I was stalling for time, he didn't show it. I suppose the thought was in my own mind.

While I waited for John to make the call from his office, I found it impossible to concentrate. Waiting makes me restless.

Someone else was restless, outside in the hall. Every now and then I saw Felix pass my door, his face drawn with worry as he looked in. When our eyes met, he hurried away, but not far. The next time he passed, I was waiting for him by the door. "Felix, do you want to see me?"

"I don't want to bother you, brother Dave," he said, hesitating in the doorway. "Maybe some other time?"

"No, Felix, trouble doesn't always wait until some other time," I said, pointing to a chair. "And you know you're not bothering me, don't you?"

"I guess so," he answered mechanically. He seemed preoccupied.

"Let's have it, Felix," I said. I closed the door, thinking he might want a little privacy.

"Doris lit out," he said, dully. "She's back on the street."

I didn't want to tell him that I knew it would happen. He would have asked why I didn't do something to stop it, and that would be hard to explain. Felix wasn't off the street long enough to understand.

"Did you hear me?" Felix asked, impatiently snapping his fingers. "Doris is gone!"

"Yes, Felix, I heard," I said. I sat down, propped my elbows on my desk, and leaned hard on them. "I can't do anything about Doris. I can only thank God that you didn't go with her. That's what she wanted, wasn't it?"

He nodded. "I told her she was crazy to go back. Dave, we could have a good life together. Maybe we could live like a real family when the baby comes." Felix shook his head and rubbed his eyes, ashamed to be seen crying. "She just couldn't dig it, that's all!"

"When did she go, Felix?"

"Last night, maybe early this morning. I'm not sure."

"How soon did she call you after she left?"

Felix looked up in surprise. "About an hour ago. How did you know?"

"I didn't," I said. "I guessed. Felix, this has happened before, many times. That's why I know I can't do anything for Doris right now. Believe me, I've tried."

Felix stood up and began to pace. "Maybe I can bring her back." He was edging toward the door.

"Sit down, Felix," I ordered. He stopped, uncertainly. "You heard me! Sit down!" His hand went for the door. "Felix, if you really believed you could help Doris, you would have gone with her. When you came up here

79

and started walking back and forth in front of my door, you were saying something you couldn't put into words. You were telling me to give you a reason to stay here, weren't you?"

Felix covered his face with his hands. "I want to stay, but I don't feel like a man if I do!" he muttered.

"Well, let me tell you a story, a true story, about another guy who felt the same way. Sit down, Felix." This time he carried out my order like an obedient child.

"Once upon a time, there was a guy, a junkie, but a real good guy, who wanted to find out how it felt to be clean again. He came to us, kicked his habit, went through the whole program, and then stayed at the farm. He was doing the whole bit; he was even thinking about going to school, and making something of himself. You see, Felix, he had a wife and a kid, a little girl, and he wanted to make up to them for all the rottenness he'd brought into their lives.

"Now this guy's wife wasn't a junkie. She was clean, and she wanted him clean, too, but she didn't understand this 'religion business' her husband got hipped on here. She was lonely, too, even though her husband used to make her life a hell on earth. So she began to put pressure on him—wrote him letters, called him up, turned on the tears when she came to see him, wouldn't bring their kid with her. She kept asking him how soon he was coming home. She got him real worked up, and finally, she had a friend call him at the farm and tell him his wife was sick and his little girl was all alone.

"So what's the guy to do? He came and talked to us, and we told him he had to make up his own mind. But we warned him. We told him to find out whether his wife was really sick before he went back to his old neighborhood. We offered to help, too, but he couldn't wait for us to ask around. He had to go and prove he was a man!"

Felix nodded. He was with me, every word of the way.

"Okay," I said. "We agree. He was good and straight, right?" Felix nodded again. "Now, let me tell you what kind of a man he proved himself to be. Can you guess where he is today?" Felix shook his head. "He's in prison, for life. He killed somebody." Felix sat up straight.

"You see, he found his wife waiting for him when he went home. She wasn't sick. You couldn't blame her; she just didn't want to be alone in the world. She figured it was better to have a junkie husband than no husband at all, and she even threw a little homecoming party for the guy. Some of his old friends were there, and a bag of heroin, too. Nice, huh?

"The guy never came back to us, Felix, and he found himself in real trouble. He couldn't hide from the truth any more. He *knew* he was doing wrong, and that put him right in the middle, between Jesus and the devil. He couldn't get up the strength to go over to one side or the other, and the pressure built up. One day, when he was dying for a fix and his little girl was crying from hunger, he cracked. He picked up his daughter, ran to a window, and threw her out. He killed her.

"When I remember this guy—and I'll never forget him, Felix—I wonder whether he felt like a man when he killed his child."

Felix was silent, and I decided that I had said enough, too. The final decision had to be his. "I'll wait awhile," he said, and got up to leave. "I really want to stay, but I can't make any promises."

"None of us can, Felix." He left just as John came in with a big smile on his face.

"Dave, I just got the most wonderful prescription!" he said. At first, I didn't understand what he meant because my thoughts went out the door with Felix. "I told the doctor about Shirley, and he agreed that she'd probably have a risky time coming off drugs. Then he gave it some thought, and he said, 'John, I think you ought to forget about any pills, and let God take care of Shirley. He's done a pretty good job over there, from what I can see!'"

My grin was as big as John's. I felt somewhat ashamed, though, because that was one prescription I should have been able to write for myself. "Thank you, Lord," I said, "for bringing up the reserves when I fell down on the job!"

I'll never know how Shirley made it as far as the Center. She was so feeble and wasted that she needed our support to climb the stairs. Had so much happened to her in only a few months? Her clothes were actually ragged now; her sensitive face was marred by ugly abscesses, and her nose ran continually; her long brown hair was dirty and hung in tangled knots that hadn't been combed for days. She was the addict at the end of her rope, "all strung out," as she put it, and she had a very practical need to come in off the street. She was too repulsive to make a living out there.

Shirley sat listlessly as John, my brother, and I began to interview her. She was perfectly agreeable to all the rules we laid down; she simply didn't have the energy to find life objectionable any more.

"When do I start prayin'?" she asked, with a faint touch of sarcasm.

"Whenever you want," Don said.

"You mean I don't have to say a prayer to get in here?" Shirley asked.

"No, Shirley," I explained. "You just have to hit bottom hard enough to want help—and I think you have."

"I gotta kick it for real this time," she said, angrily. Her voice broke from weakness. "I want to be clean when my old man comes out of jail. And I want to get my kids back from the welfare department. I'm gonna make them tell me where my kids are!" She looked from one of us to the other, as if seeking some kind of approval.

I pushed the telephone toward her. "Here, Shirley, let's call the welfare department, and ask them where your children are."

"What do you mean? You tryin' to game me?" She drew her head back and squinted at me. Her eyes were dark and sunken.

"No, I'm leveling with you. Go ahead, make your call. I'll look up the number for you."

She didn't reach for the phone.

"Do you want me to call for you? What's the name of the social worker in charge of your case?"

She dropped her head, and I couldn't see her eyes.

"You don't really know, do you, Shirley?" I asked. I knew we had to be severe, even though the girl was obviously very ill. "The welfare department didn't take those children away from you, did they? You wanted to get them off your hands because you were killing them with neglect. Isn't that the way it happened?"

"Yes," she whined in a voice we could barely hear. "They made me sign some papers so I couldn't get my kids back."

"That's a lie, Shirley. We looked into your records, and they tell a different story, a story of a mother who refused to come and see her children after she asked the welfare department to take care of them." Shirley shrugged her shoulders. "It's almost impossible for anyone to take a child away from his mother, Shirley, and the welfare department doesn't even try. But you *did* sign a paper giving them temporary custody of your children, isn't that right?" She nodded. "And didn't that paper give you the right to remove them from their foster home whenever you wanted them?"

"Yes."

"Then why didn't you ever go to see your children? You kept promising the social worker that you would."

Shirley took a deep breath and sighed. "Don't you understand how it is with a junkie?" she asked. "I wanted my kids, yet I didn't want them. I don't know why. All I know is that I was afraid I would do something to them if I kept them around. Sometimes I get nervous, sometimes I can't get a fix, and when a kid starts cryin' I never know what I'll do."

Shirley had shown her love for her children in the only way an addict can: by giving them up. That was the truth I hoped she would see someday, but first she had to give up her lie about losing the children.

"I understand now, Shirley," I said. "I really do."

The interview ended, and Elsie Benton came to take Shirley "home." "I'll have to look through your purse, Shirley," John said. "I might as well be blunt about it. We don't trust junkies here." He was looking for "insurance," that little emergency supply of drugs addicts sometimes tried to smuggle in with them. They never intended to use it, they all claimed, but we knew better.

A faintly mocking smile spread across Shirley's face. "I'm sorry, Reverend Benton," she said, softly, "I don't have one." She fumbled in a pocket of her skirt for a moment. "I guess these are the only things I own," she said, pulling out some torn facial tissues. In all, she had three of them.

Shirley suffered through withdrawal, but so far there were no convulsions. During her first few days at the Center, her only complaint was her lack of privacy. Although we had entrusted to God, we didn't think we ought to sit back and forget about her, and I'm afraid we overdid the tender love and care.

"How many shows am I supposed to give today?" she growled when I stopped at the girls' home to see how she was doing. I didn't mind her grumpiness; if she felt up to complaining, it was a pretty favorable sign that her physical ordeal was over.

"What am I, some kind of a freak?" she went on. "I thought you people were used to seeing junkies!" She wasn't really angry, and I saw a gleam of humor in her eyes.

"Well, you're an exceptional one," I said. "We never saw one as bedraggled as you were."

She was about to say something, and decided against it. Almost reluctantly, she smiled. "How *about* that!" she said, genuinely pleased with herself, "Not a pill, not a shot, nothing! And no complications!" She held out her hand. "Thanks. It never went this way before, honest."

I shook her hand. "Thank Somebody Else, Shirley, not us. We only prayed. Christ did all the work."

87

"That reminds me," she said. "What time am I supposed to be in chapel?"

"Ten-thirty," I said glancing at my watch. "And that reminds *me*—it's almost that time."

"I really want to go," she said, and seemed embarrassed. "Don't get me wrong. I'm not gonna burst into prayer, or anything like that. I just want to see what goes on there." She laughed. "I want to see if I'm strong enough to take it."

Our chapel at 416 Clinton Avenue is a plain, large room, and we sit on folding chairs. Nothing is fancy, which is sometimes a letdown to our new converts. They can't understand why someone as powerful as God doesn't live it up a little. "You ought to jazz up the place, y'know?" was the advice of one of our recent arrivals. After a while, they begin to appreciate the chapel's simplicity; it doesn't draw their attention away from God.

Shirley stopped at the chapel door. She felt strange and new, and I thought she might have lost her nerve. She hadn't; she walked in and took an empty chair next to Margarita. Chickie and Eva were in the same row, and the girls turned and nodded to each other. It was more than a greeting. In one moment, something sinister came over them, and when they looked around I saw it in their eyes. They all came from the same dark, humiliating way of life, and their sins seemed to unite them. A sisterhood of rebellion was forming right before our eyes, closing its ranks on our love, and we couldn't do a thing to stop it.

The four young women sat icily throughout the service. Eva didn't even move her lips to pretend she was praying. Something had gone wrong. Our converts usually gained strength from the knowledge that they all had a chance to build a new life; this sisterhood of rebellion seemed to be toughened by their common doom. I was shocked by the thought that three of these girls were mothers, and among them they had seven children. Seven little people! My list of lost children was already growing too fast. Would I soon have to add so many new names?

When the service ended and we knelt to pray, one of the boys began to moan and sob as he cried out, "Jesus! Forgive me, Jesus!" It was Julio, a boy who had come to us about two weeks ago, convinced that he was beyond saving. "Jesus didn't know any guys like me when He talked about forgiveness," he used to say.

Don got up and went to him, kneeling beside him and joining in prayer with him. "This boy means it, Jesus. Let him know that You mean it, too. Let him know soon, Jesus! Today!"

I heard a familiar scornful laugh and looked up. Shirley was standing near them. "Oh, what a good little boy!" she taunted, pointing to Julio and laughing again. I saw the boy's back stiffen with anger, but he wouldn't raise his head. He didn't want a girl to see the tears running down his cheeks.

I couldn't get my mind off the four young women I had watched in chapel that morning. I was especially concerned about Margarita because she was so much younger than the others. There was very little that she did not already know about sin, but I didn't want her to have a chance to learn it now. Somehow, I had to break up the sisterhood.

9

In a way, I was faced with Jose's problem all over again, but it was even harder to solve for a girl. No matter how many people may still carry on the battle of the sexes, the girls had undoubtedly won it in the field of crime; they began their criminal activities at a much earlier age than the boys, and they learned incredibly fast. When girls were admitted to foster homes, they were disruptive influences on any boys living there; they could teach them too many ways to break the rules. Most of the children's homes, both public and private, therefore housed the girls in separate buildings.

In spite of my determination to assume responsibility for Jose, I hadn't made any encouraging contacts. No one seemed to know how to help him. I was afraid I would have no better success with inquiries about a home for Margarita, and reluctantly I found myself thinking once more of going to the children's bureau of the welfare department.

The outlook was very discouraging. There were so many little people like Jose and Margarita; they would soon become big people, bitter and hopeless, and no one seemed willing to offer them a better kind of life. They were like the older children I had seen in children's homes, the ones who were called "unadoptable," not because there was anything wrong with them, but because their age made them seem like used or second-hand children.

Even if their parents agreed to release them for adoption, which they surely would not do, Jose and Margarita would have little chance of being adopted. Most adoptive parents want to start out with a brand new human being, a baby they can mold to fit in with their way of life. Older children already have a way of life, and they have problems, too; they're a challenge more than a blessing, and so they are passed by and left to handle their tremendous problems all by themselves. Ironically, they get stuck with the challenge many adults consider too tough for them.

The lack of adoptions wasn't the only reason why some boys and girls spent most of their young lives in "temporary" institutional homes. Perhaps they might have been adopted when they were younger, if only their natural parents had agreed to it. But many slum parents couldn't give up their children, even if they were unable to make a home for them. The story had become disturbingly familiar; a mother who drank or took drugs, a father who never existed; an occasional meeting between mother and child in an institutional visiting room, a tearful parting, and the same old promises of "I'll come and get you, Honey, soon as I can get a job." Finally, the story ended when the child became old enough to leave the home and get his own job.

I had seen some of the public-supported homes for girls, and they were more attractive than the boys' homes. Even in a large institution, the feminine talent for homemaking strikes a vistor the moment he enters the front door. There are more pictures on the walls, and the cutout paper flowers burst out of the dormitories and into the halls and the administrative offices. Color is everywhere, and it isn't all "institutional" green, either. In the dormitories you can see that a lot of thought has been given to what goes with what, and while neatness is still the most important feature of these rooms, it is softened by a feeling of harmony, and even a touch of gaiety here and there in the form of a bright, hand-stitched pillow carefully propped up on a bed.

I guess girls like a little more privacy than boys do, because closets in the girls' dorms have doors. In the few that were open to view, I saw more changes of clothes than the boys usually had, and the quality of the clothes was generally quite good. This wasn't surprising, because girls of Margarita's age and background were quite self-sufficient. They could stroll through a department store and come out with a stolen wardrobe; they were very fashion-conscious, too, and didn't waste their time stealing anything but the highest-priced merchandise. Eventually they sold what they stole, but only after they had worn most of the things a few times.

I wondered how Margarita would get along with a

lot of other girls. For the past two years, she had lived a wild life out in the street, never sleeping or eating at home. As she said, she slipped in the door when her mother went out, and only to change her clothes.

It wouldn't be fair, I decided. I had been shocked by the sly worldliness I saw in the faces of some very young girls in the institutions I visited. How could we send a girl like Margarita to live among them? She would become their heroine, their idol; she would be able to answer the questions that never should have come into their heads. They would ask her how it felt to shoot it up, to get high. How does a girl get started as a pusher? They would want to know. How does she approach a man she wants to hustle? What are the prostituting facts of life?

No, by removing Margarita from the dangerous influence of her new and more experienced friends, we would be passing her on as a dangerous influence to still younger girls. We couldn't try to save Margarita at their expense. We would have to let her take her chances among the sisterhood of rebellion and pray that God Himself could somehow break down their unholy defiance.

You can talk to an addict until you're blue in the face, but he won't believe a word you say. It takes a converted addict to reach another addict, just as it took a converted gang member to reach the others. Our staff knew all the junkie lingo, all the addicts' routines, their fears and weaknesses, and we realized that the odds were ninety-eight percent against them when it came to kicking their habit. Still, we couldn't always get through to them with a word of hope. As they saw it, we were "squares," people who had always been clean. It didn't matter whether our hearts broke for every junkie we saw; we had never broken the skin on our arms with a dirty, perhaps contaminated, needle. We were outsiders.

We didn't *know* how it was *to be* an addict, but our converts did, and we were glad to find that most of them were eager to go back onto the street and talk about it. They were walking proof that a drug habit could be kicked, and they could explain why drying out was a process that had to go soul-deep.

We always tried to take some of our converts along when we went out to do street work. We knew it was useless to tell an addict that he could be cured; we had to show him. He had to hear the words from a guy who used to nod on the same street corner. Then he began to listen.

It takes a long time after that to bring an addict into the Center. Our words have to start eating away at him; he has to wake up with them on his mind, and try running away from them day after day. He has to tell himself that he comes back night after night to the same street corner just to laugh at us, but he keeps coming back all the same. He has to ask us questions, pin us down, try to trick us into contradicting ourselves; and all this time he's silently begging to believe we're telling the truth. An addict doesn't give in to God easily; you see, he's suspicious of anyone who wants to save him, because he can't believe he's worth saving. So he tries to hold God off at arm's length, and yet he doesn't want to let go of Him entirely. If he holds on long enough, he becomes exhausted; he gives up, gives in, and discovers that the love he has fought and distrusted is genuine, after all. He knows he hasn't earned it and he isn't worthy of it, but he realizes that no one else is, either. This isn't a give-and-take kind of love; it's a blessing. It's "give" all the way.

Our converts see plenty of little people, especially the *very* little ones, because they get into places some of us don't often see; they know where to look for junkies. Sometimes their old buddies ask them to come to their homes and talk to them about their chances of getting clean; and while our converts know as well as the rest of us that addicts don't usually keep appointments, they always try to go. They see a lot of infants that way, although they usually see them in the most shocking and distressing conditions.

The very little people are the babies, the one-, two-, and three-year-old infants of the big people who live in the city's poorest, most rundown areas. They live and breathe misery from the time they are born, and although their death rate is high, I'm amazed that any of them survive.

It's hard to talk to the very little people because they understand so few words. An addicted mother doesn't have the time or the patience to sit down with a child and carefully form her lips into words; she teaches her child to *shut up* and *get out,* and her methods are curses and blows.

Who feeds these very little ones? Sometimes they do not eat. Sometimes they are left with a sympathetic neighbor while "mother runs out for a minute"; but when that minute turns into several days, the neighbors begin to run out of sympathy. Then the child may be left alone, because mother's nursing a habit, not a baby, and if it should cry for hours, or possibly days, who will notice? So many babies cry in tenement country.

A junkie mother isn't heartless. She'll be the first to tell you that she's bad for her kid. She'll cry in shame for the things she has done to her baby; and if that baby should die from her neglect, she'll never forgive herself. Her guilt, in fact, will drive her straight back to the needle, perhaps in the hope that she will accidentally take an overdose and die.

When a junkie mother slams out of her apartment, closing her ears to the wailing sounds of her child, she really intends to take some food back with her when she goes home. The trouble is, she often doesn't go home in time, and the baby may starve to death.

It also takes an addict a long time to get enough money to feed the baby. First, she has to go out and hustle; if she's been a prostitute for a long time, she can work fast, but if she's new at her job, she wastes a lot of time soliciting the wrong people. By the time she "turns a trick" or two, as the hustlers call their work, her nerves are screaming for a fix, and the baby just has to wait while mama "takes off." Once the drug shoots through her system, she cares about nothing in the world—not her baby, its hunger, or its terror of being alone. Man, this gal is high, and *nothing* can touch her!

Our workers see some hungry, dirty, frightened little people when they go to addicts' homes. Most of the time, they find the babies alone, and it is hard for any of us to obey the law and leave them where they are; we have no legal right to take them away. We can give them something to eat, and bathe their frail bodies, and wrap them in clean blankets, and pray for them, little more. Only the parents of the very little people can bring them in to us.

Two infants were brought to us early in November. They were two little girls: Ruth, three years old, and Virginia, less than a year. They were the daughters of a woman named Joan, an addict well known to two of our converts, who used to get high with her when they were hooked. Joan had been promising her two friends that she would come to the Center one of these days, but she began to back away. Finally, she stopped coming to the street meetings, until she suddenly reappeared one night, pale, thin, and obviously in great pain. "I'm sick," she gasped, "but I think my kids are dead!" Her friends turned her over to the care of the other members of the street team while they hurried to her apartment. They found the children alive, but they saw why Joan thought they were dead. They were in a state of shock.

Joan was a girl who believed she could kick her drug habit by herself, and whenever she pleased. Periodically, she would con a neighbor into taking care of her children while she locked herself in a borrowed room and tried to do without her fix. Withdrawal is like a severe case of the flu; its symptoms are constant vomiting, stomach cramps, and diarrhea, and in most cases they last for two or three days. The physical symptoms, while uncomfortable, cannot be compared to the terrible emotional and mental tortures an addict suffers on his way back to the real world. Every ugly detail of his life suddenly hits him full in the face; all of the wretchedness he had tried to forget happens to him, as if for the first time, and he is too weak to fight it off. His senses begin to function again, and he recalls most bitterly that he is a hated, abandoned, useless human being, a piece of the world's trash that has somehow slipped out of its proper container. These are the experiences that Joan made herself suffer periodically, and when she came out of her locked room she made a beeline for a pusher.

On one of those days when she decided to kick her habit—probably because she was dead broke and too sick to get any money—she couldn't find a neighbor she could con. They were wise to her. So she went back to her apartment and convinced herself that her children didn't have to stand in her way. She could kick her habit and manage to take care of them, she told herself.

This time, something went wrong. Joan began to realize that she was ill with something more than withdrawal. She had never felt so feeble, so faint. Her two little girls were in a crib, and she pulled it close to the stove so that when she fed them, she wouldn't have to take so many steps. Then she lit the burner under a kettle of water, thinking a cup of tea might pick her up, and staggered back to her bed. She passed out.

Children, of course, are curious, and Joan's oldest daughter sat watching the steaming kettle as long as she could. Then she stood in the crib and reached toward the kettle, upsetting it so that its boiling contents splashed into the crib onto the sleeping infant, who screamed in agony, and onto the feet of the horrified older girl. When Joan regained consciousness, she found the children lying in the crib, eyes wide open and staring at the ceiling.

I saw little Ruth and Virginia when our street team brought them to the Center, and I'm not ashamed to say that I wept. They had been treated for scalds and shock, but the marks of their mother's neglect left them in a condition I could describe only with tears. The diapers on the younger infant hadn't been changed in days, and her filthy, bony little body was covered with ugly sores. In her wispy black hair we found lice, and there was caked dirt in the creases of skin at her wrists, neck, and ankles. Ruth, the older girl, wore only torn, dirty cotton underwear, much too small for her, and her arms were red and sore from the chafing of the sleeves. She, too, was filthy and lice-ridden. Both children smelled foul and sour, and that made me angry as well as sick. Babies are supposed to smell sweet by nature; someone incredibly cruel had destroyed the scent of childhood in these two baby girls.

Joan was ill with a virus infection, and too weak to leave. She and her two girls were to stay with us until they were well. The girls on our staff were eager to nurse the babies back to health, and within a few days we began to see the results of their dedication. Little Ruth was skipping all around the Center, and baby Virginia grinned at everyone she saw. We called them "the miracle babies."

Joan's arrival at the Center had been dramatic, but more or less accidental. She hadn't come because she decided she needed help, and she wasn't likely to stay around until she got some. When she was strong enough, she would be on her way, and her children would probably go with her.

We hoped we could hold onto the children for a little while. Joan claimed that she had nothing in the world except her girls, but maybe she would realize that they had nothing at all. They desperately needed the nourishment of a loving home and healthy parents.

If we could persuade Joan to give up her children, even temporarily, who would take them? I thought of the nursery in a welfare home I had visited, so immaculate but so crowded. Infants made up the largest group of children who were brought to the public-supported homes, and space on the nursery floor was a serious problem. Sometimes the cribs had to be moved into the hallways during the day to clear a play area for children old enough to walk.

I remembered being taken through the orderly rows

of clean white cribs, and stopping now and then to look down at a tiny head, so dark against the sparkling whiteness of the linens. It was nap time, and the sounds of rapid baby-breathing seemed to make my own breath catch in my throat.

Infants need a great deal of care, and the staff of the nursery floor were doing more than their normal share of work. If only they could acquire a new building, said the official who was showing me through the home; with another building, they could at least be prepared for the many more babies they knew would come in the months and years ahead. But the city can't simply go out and buy or construct a building, as private agencies can. In a city like New York, there aren't any vacant lots, and a builder usually has to tear down an old building before he can put up a new one. The city has an additional problem because it can only buy land that has been legally condemned, and condemnation proceedings can go on for years in the courts. They can also light political fires. As far as the crowded nursery was concerned, "We'll make room for them, somehow," the welfare official sighed. "You can't turn your back on a baby, can you?"

Apparently, some people could, and did. But surely I would not find closed doors or turned backs in any of the religious homes for children. I had hesitated to ask them to help our little people because I assumed they were already handling as many children as they could accommodate. Now I had to go to them. We needed homes for four children—Jose, Margarita, and Joan's two daughters—and if they existed anywhere in the City of New York, I had to find them.

The director of the children's home shifted uncomfortably in his chair when I repeated my question: "Why aren't these children given religious training?" I couldn't understand why the curriculum of a church-supported children's home didn't include Bible-study courses.

"Well, Mr. Wilkerson, I have to speak bluntly," he said. "Religion isn't going to help these kids."

"I can't believe that," I said. I was aware that I sounded indignant, but that's the way I felt. I didn't expect such words from anyone in a religious institution.

"I don't *like* to believe it," he said gently, as if he wanted to spare me the harshness of reality as he saw it. "But it's true. Church doesn't mean a thing to these kids, and they'd laugh at us if we tried to make them study the Bible." He settled back in his chair. "Our children have deep, disturbing problems. They come from troubled families. We have to reach them in ways they can accept."

"What ways?"

"There are many. We have a trained psychiatrist on our staff, plus a recreational therapist, and a vocational guidance director. We try to determine the emotional needs of each child—."

I didn't intend to seem rude, but I couldn't restrain myself. "What about the needs of their souls?" I interrupted. He frowned and shook his head sympathetically. "Mr. Wilkerson, we just aren't equipped for that sort of therapy." Who was, I wondered, if the church itself was not?

I had no right to blame this man because he could not answer my call for help. He was telling me the same thing I had heard from church members in all parts of the country: "We want to help, *but*—."

The children admitted to this institution lived more comfortably than those in the public foster homes. There was much more space for each child, but I didn't like the reason for it. I saw empty beds, more than the four my little people needed, and only a few to each dormitory; there were bureaus and desks as well as closets, and each child had a decent supply of clothes. The rooms were very neat, just like the others I had seen, and wherever I looked I saw personal belongings —books, toys, games, photographs. These children had ties to the outside world; they were not like our little people.

I was told that the emphasis in the home was on scholastic achievement. "Generally, our children do very well in their studies," a staff member said as we looked in on one of the classrooms. It was as though I were watching an ordinary group of school children whose mothers had kissed them goodbye and sent them on their way that morning. None of them had that beaten, wasted look of the little people.

"Do any of these children come from the slums?" I asked.

"A few," my guide answered. "We accept children on the basis of their ability to keep up with our educational standards, and, unfortunately, very few slum children can do that. Most of them do badly in school, and they would only hold back our other children. Besides, they have some pretty serious emotional problems."

That left our four kids out in the cold. According to these "standards," they would have torn the place apart. I had to admit that everything this man said was true. The little people get the worst possible grades in school, if the school manages to put up with them at all, and they have no control over their emotions. If someone hurts them, they strike back ferociously, no matter what the risk to themselves.

No, my kids would never qualify for the empty beds in this home. They would have to be filled by the more acceptable children, the ones who could keep up with the high educational standards, and perhaps even surpass them, the ones who would be able to make something of themselves and prove to the contributing church members that their investment was really doing some good.

Our little people were hard to work with, and they weren't likely to thank us for anything we did for them. They weren't convinced they needed our love or our understanding, not after doing without them for so many years, and they took their time accepting them. Just when we thought we were getting somewhere, they might say, "Thank you, Buddy," and take one fast slide back into misery. At least they knew their way around there, whereas they might not be quite sure of their footing in our world.

We didn't expect great things of our little people. We didn't look forward to a day when they would make us proud of them, when we could point to them as statistics of our success. If they took one hesitant step forward, it was almost a miracle, and God deserved the credit for it.

A church-supported home for children has to consider a lot of things that never concern us at Teen Challenge, and in that sense we were spoiled. We didn't have to worry about showing the "right" kind of results. I sympathized with such problems, but I couldn't agree with a philosophy that claimed the church didn't mean a thing to the troubled children I saw. I'm afraid I began to believe it was the other way around, and that the troubled children of our world didn't mean anything to the church.

I was terribly discouraged. The words I had heard about the church and its relationship to the children burned into my mind all the next day. I went over them again and again, thinking I might have misinterpreted them, and I didn't really seem to hear the excited chatter going on around me. We were on our way to a youth rally in Pittsburgh, which was the greatest distance our girls had ever traveled.

12

We were in our station wagon, and Don was driving. Margarita, Eva, and Anna sat in the middle seat, twitching around, trying to look out both sides at once. Chickie sat glumly in the back, not saying a word. The more the other girls giggled and pointed, the more Chickie frowned, as if she wanted to be sure her disapproval was noticed.

I was sitting up front with Don, staring out the window but paying very little attention to the landscape. Now and then, I glanced up at the rear-view mirror, where I could see Chickie's reflection. She was building up to something.

I wondered what the average congregation would say about Chickie's baby. What would they do if such a child were left on their doorstep? Would they be able to tell, just by looking at him, that the boy's mother was a hardened criminal, a woman who had been the most violent, incorrigible patient in a prison-hospital mental ward? Would they walk around such a child, keeping at a safe distance, if they knew that he came from a home where privacy was unknown, and children were squeezed in with adults with no regard to what they saw? This was the kind of child most people said they wanted to help, yet so many of them withheld their hands. Were they afraid he would dirty them? Was his shame, his need, contagious? This baby belonged in the midst of the church; it needed to feel the nearness and strength of people who bent their knees in prayer. Did only the "nice" children from the "nice" homes get into church these days?

Who was supposed to take care of the little people? Was the church afraid it would be infected by the sickness they had picked up at the bottom of the world? Why was it afraid? A church that is strong in the love of God has nothing to fear; it can safely nourish the most abused of sin's children. But if a church has drifted from its mission in the world, then I can understand its fears. Jesus said, ". . . whosoever shall offend one of these little ones . . . , it is better for him that a millstone were hanged about his neck, and he were cast into the sea" (Mark 9:42). Well, turning away from the little people was certainly a way of offending them.

"Oh, God," I prayed, "I don't know whether I'm right in the way I'm going. I've got to have some sign, some clue, from You. Is there a way to help the little people? Is it too late, God? Please let me know, in some way I can understand!"

The vast auditorium where our rally was held was filled to capacity with a few thousand teen-agers. The lights were bright, and the voices before the service began were loud and excited. I wondered how many of these eager, curious, hopeful young people would slip away from us this time. They had so many excuses for sidestepping the Christ they desperately needed. I was tired of excuses.

"Did you come here to get bugged by a sermon?" I asked. I could see the heads jerk up in surprise and the smiles began to fade. "Did you come to shed a few tears? Are you going to come forward and 'decide' for Christ, and then say a nice little prayer in private? Is this going to ease your conscience?

"What's a 'conscience,' anyway? Do any of you know? Conscience is part of your personality. It was given to you by God when He created you, and He gave it to you for a practical purpose. It's a very handy gadget, this conscience of ours. God designed it to 'smile' when we do the right things, and that's a great feeling. We all like to have it. We don't like it when our conscience 'frowns'; that means we've done something wrong. But we've managed to get around the frowns. We've tampered with our consciences, and now they don't know right from wrong. Everything looks the same to them, and that makes it easier for us to do as we please.

"Let's get one thing straight. Unless you're letting God call the shots in your life, you're a rebel against Him. You want your own way, and you want no part of His, except to blame Him for all the bad things that happen to you. But the blame goes straight back to you, and don't think you can pass it on to your parents, either. Maybe they weren't the best influences in the world, but you've got a will of your own. If your life isn't going in the right direction, you can still turn it around. You can stop being your own little god, and turn your life over to the one real God."

I heard a scream from the back of the hall, and faces turned away from me to see what was happening. "Oh, Jesus! Help me up!" I heard a girl cry, and two thin arms reached up into the air. It was Chickie. She stood on her toes, stretching her arms higher and higher, as if she were trying to reach a hand held out to her from above. Her face sparkled in the distance, and I realized that it must have been wet with tears. Chickie was crying! The girl who boasted that she was too hard to cry had given in!

Later, Don and I knelt with her in a small chapel off the large hall. I had a special prayer to offer, but not only for Chickie's acceptance of a Saviour, but for God's answer to my earlier prayer. I had wanted some kind of a sign, and Chickie's breaking point was one I couldn't miss. I hadn't been able to get any help for the little people so far, but I was going to keep trying. God evidently didn't want me to call it quits.

The sisterhood of rebellion was losing a member. Chickie was joining the other side, God's side, and I knew it wouldn't be long before the others would follow. Chickie was determined to work on them. "They've got to learn what I learned," she said, on the way back to Brooklyn. "They've got to feel loved!"

It's a good thing Chickie offered us some encouragement that day, because when we returned to the Center late at night I took one look at John's face and braced myself. "What's the matter?" I asked.

Whatever it was, John took it personally. His normally happy face was lined with worry. "It's Shirley," he said. "I don't know how it happened, or why. She's gone." I understood what he was thinking; first Doris, now Shirley; we had lost two mothers, and possibly four children.

"It figures," I said. "She was getting restless."

"That's not the worst of it," John said. "Guess who went with her?" He didn't wait for my answer. "Julio," he said.

"Julio!" Apart from the morning in the chapel, when Shirley ridiculed Julio for dropping to his knees, I didn't realize they knew each other. Of course, they didn't need a formal introduction. They both were addicts, and that made them buddies before a word was spoken. I could imagine how it happened. Shirley probably got an appetite for a fix, and instead of coming to any of the staff and talking about it, she fell back on a more familiar solution. She wandered over to the cafeteria, where she could count on finding some boys; she knew they would be vulnerable to an invitation. Most people seem to think that addicts are sexually benumbed by their habit, but this is true *only as long as they are high.* Let them come off the nod, and watch out! Their normal sexual desires, long repressed by narcotics, return suddenly and with an accumulated force that strains at any control.

Shirley had an easy time. "I'm ready to blow this joint," was all she had to say, and she had company for the journey back to hell. She just happened to pick on Julio, and he didn't have a chance.

"She was doing so well, Dave," Don said. "I really thought she was going to make it."

I tried to encourage him, but there was no use telling him he would get used to this sort of heartbreak. If you're the kind whose heart breaks, that's all there is to it.

Later, John remembered something; he thought he had discovered why Shirley had run away. She had wanted to see her little girl, and John had gone with her to her mother's apartment. "The baby wasn't there, Dave," he told me. "Shirley's mother had passed her on to a neighbor because she didn't want to be bothered with her any more. She was dead drunk when we saw her, and Shirley got very upset. I didn't think we should go to the neighbor's apartment, but she insisted. It was the wrong thing to do. The woman and her husband were just as drunk as Shirley's mother, and— honest, Dave, I was afraid they were going to drop that baby every time they picked her up!"

"How did the baby look?"

"Well enough. I guess she's getting enough food, and these people seem to fuss over her. They're not poor; they've got enough money to take care of her and still buy their liquor, but, well—."

"I know, John. One of these days they might pass out and leave a cigarette burning. That's a rotten way to love a kid!"

"Shirley didn't say a word while we were there. She even seemed to hold back from looking at her little girl. I don't know what she was thinking, but on the way home she began to talk about getting well enough to take care of her daughter. I think she really meant it, Dave."

"I do, too. And maybe that's why she went back onto

the street. She wasn't ready to take on so much responsibility, and she knew it. It just scared her off."

"But why didn't she come and tell us about it?" Don wondered. "We could have helped her."

I understood how Don felt. It's a sad moment in our ministry when a rebellious soul flees back into darkness without giving us a decent chance to get through to it with a flicker of light. The sisterhood had lost another member, but to the wrong side.

"You wanted to see me?" Joan slouched in the doorway.

"Yes, and you're late," I said abruptly, "But come in, and sit down."

Joan's face had filled out in the two weeks she had been with us, although there was no change in her expression; she was still preoccupied. She sat in a chair facing my desk and stared out the window behind me.

"How long has it been since you saw your children, Joan?" I asked. Reluctantly, I had had to burden the welfare department with my problem, and they came up with a good solution. They had arranged to put Joan's two little girls in a private foster home until we could make more permanent arrangements for them. I was hoping I could persuade Joan to give them up for adoption, and thereby give them a chance in life.

Joan didn't even blink her eyes. "Couple of days, I guess. You know how it is, man. I just can't remember things like that."

"Your children aren't 'things like that,' Joan. They should be the most important people in your whole life—more important than yourself."

She turned her head slowly and looked at me thoughtfully. "You know a junkie can't think that way, Brother Dave. You've made the scene; you see the way it is with us."

115

"You're not a junkie now, Joan. You've been clean for two weeks." Much as I tried, I couldn't bring myself to believe that Joan was going to stay clean. I knew what was going on behind that faraway look in her eyes. She was homesick for her habit; she felt like a martyr because she thought she was giving up something good. Until she looked at drugs as something repulsive, she would never be able to give them up.

It was time to get to the point. "Why don't you give Ruth and Virginia up for adoption, Joan?" I asked. Now I had her full attention. "They're still very young, and there are so many childless couples who could offer them a wonderful life."

"No deal!" Joan snapped. "Let me tell you something. When I knew I was going to have a kid, I was happy—in a stupid sort of way! Don't think I had to have children. Don't think I didn't know what to do if I wanted to get rid of them!"

"Why were you happy? Didn't you wonder how you'd take care of them?"

Joan stood up and leaned over my desk, pressing her forefinger down on it to emphasize her point. "Do you know what I was thinkin' this mornin'? I said to myself, 'Joan, it's about time you got up in the mornin' and tried to remember what day of the week it is!' Now, I got to try real hard to do that one little thing, 'cause I'm not in the habit of thinkin' about nothin' any more. And you expect a junkie to plan how she's goin' to take care of a kid? You know us better than that. I love my kids, but I gotta live one day at a time!"

I wasn't getting anywhere. "Joan, you still can't take care of your girls. You know that."

"I need my kids!"

"They need love! You can't give them that!"

"I love my kids!" she shouted. "Nobody can say I don't love my kids! If you try to take them away from me, I swear I'll go right out and get high!"

"You'll go out and get high anyway! That's what I'm trying to make you understand. Joan, I can't take your girls away from you, but I'm praying you'll give them up."

She wouldn't. I knew that, even though she promised to think about it. She had a right to visit her two little girls in their temporary foster home any time she wished, yet she couldn't bring herself to do it. There were many reasons.

Addicted mothers hated themselves for the suffering they inflicted on their children, but if they admitted their guilt, they would then have to do something about it; at least, that was the normal course of events in the life of a normal person. An addict is certainly not a normal person; an addict plays hide-and-seek with life, and while he keeps breaking its rules, he pretends it just isn't so. In that way, he thinks he can avoid the penalties. Ask any addict about his habit, and he'll talk about it as if it's something naughty, that's all. Ask one of our converts, and he'll give you the real story.

The relief money destitute mothers could collect for their babies was another good reason for Joan to hold onto her girls. Each and every month she probably planned to spend each penny of her relief money on them, but when she got the check in her hands, her mind was blinded by other necessities. "I would have left them for a month, if it meant me gettin' a shot of dope," she had told one of our workers.

Joan had another very complicated reason for keeping her daughters. They were her proof that she was a woman; they represented her softness, her dependence, her earnest need for a man. When she had to go out on the street to get money; when she had to come home by the back way so that her junkie men friends wouldn't beat her up and take it away from her; when the father of her children said, "Tough luck, honey, they're your problem!" and walked out on her, she could look at her children and say that, in spite of it all, she was a woman! Someday, she told herself, she would meet a man who would marry her and take care of her; then she could stop being so hard.

Joan's reasons had nothing to do with her children's well-being. They were related to her own needs, and they were all wrong.

John and Elsie Benton had opened their home to foster children several times over the years, and I asked them whether any of those children had missed their real parents. "Yes, at first," Elsie said, "but only because we were strangers to them and they didn't know what to expect from us."

"They had a lot of trouble with discipline," John commented. "That's something most of them didn't get in their real homes, and they didn't like it at first. They wanted to do as they pleased, and they weren't used to having any authority over them."

"How did they feel after a while?" I asked.

"Great! Once they understood that love was the reason we disciplined them, they were fine," John said.

Now I knew where the little people really belonged, if only they could get there. They suffered from a lack of real love; their parents hadn't known it, and so they couldn't give it to the children. The word *love* was used a lot, but it was only a word; it couldn't be defined in terms of actions. Children aren't fooled by parents who tell them how much they love them. They want to be shown; they want to know that someone cares how they're going to grow up, that someone will take the trouble to keep them from doing wrong.

The little people might have a chance for a decent future if they could find homes with adults who put their love into everyday living. They needed to learn about love from adults who learned it from God.

Doris was putting pressure on Felix. Her baby was due in a few weeks, and she kept calling Felix, pleading with him to meet her somewhere outside the Center. She promised to come back with him, but Felix knew better than to believe her.

14

"I don't know how long I can keep saying 'no.'" he said. He was irritable lately, and we knew he was under a terrible strain. "She sounds bad, real bad."

"I may seem cruel, Felix," I said to him, "but if she's as bad as she sounds, she'll come here."

"If she lives that long," he grunted. If anything were to happen to Doris, Felix would bear the pain; he was learning the inside story of responsibility.

I was concerned about some of the girls at the Center. Joan was our greatest disappointment. She still wanted to prove that she could take care of herself and her children, too; she had rented a dingy two-room apartment about two blocks away from the Center, where she could be on her own right under our noses. I didn't like it, but I couldn't stop her from leaving us. Her mind was on one thing, heroin, and pretty soon she would get her hands on it, too. I saw her now and then in the neighborhood, and so did most of our workers, but at no time could we be sure that she was high. Joan had a detached attitude even when she was clean.

Eva had brought on a crisis in discipline, which reminded me that I intended to have a talk with her. I had been putting it off, because I knew what I would finally have to say to her. Don and I had agreed that Eva should be dismissed.

I think she knew what was coming when she came into my office. Her smile was forced and artificial, and she wasted time by admiring my hand-me-down furniture.

"Eva, you've been giving us a lot of trouble," I began.

"Oh, I don't blame you for gettin' mad at me," she interrupted. "My whole family's down on me for the things I do. I jus' can't help myself, Brother Dave!"

"Now, Eva, I heard this same line from you when you came here a few months ago, and it's still a lie," I said. Her attitude was her problem; she seemed to enjoy lying too much to see that there was anything wrong with it.

Eva had gone home for a weekend only a few days ago, and until then we thought she was coming along fairly well. She was a clever girl who probably would have done well in language courses if she had had the opportunity to enroll in them; she could pick up words and phrases quickly and repeat them with such sincerity that we couldn't always be sure they weren't coming from her heart. Her tears came easily, too, but with such deep sobs that we had no reason to doubt them. We attributed them to her highly emotional personality.

Most of our converts get a longing for home after they have spent a few weeks with us, and although we wish they wouldn't subject themselves to the lures of the old neighborhood so early in their rehabilitation, we have to let them go. We have no hold over them, other than their willingness to take the help we offer them. Eva was unusual in that she didn't want to go home after the first few weeks; in fact, she said she never wanted to go home again. "I'll take one look at my husband puttin' a bottle up to his lips, and I'll run to the nearest pusher," she said then. Time gradually changed Eva's feelings about her husband, and she began to miss him. After she talked to him several times on the telephone, she even spoke a bit hopefully about him. Perhaps she could persuade him to come to the Center, she reasoned. We had heard those words before, and we were afraid she was heading for trouble, so we tried to talk her out of going home. We had seen converts go back for someone they had left behind, and they usually didn't return.

Eva surprised us by showing up for chapel on the Monday after her weekend at home. She looked very smug as she took a seat in the front row, somewhere she never dared to sit. I was sitting a few rows behind her, next to Don, and we both sighed in relief. Then I noticed something strange about Eva. I could only see the back of her head from where I sat, but it told me that she was flying high. Try as she did, she couldn't keep her head erect, and down it would go, coming up again with a jerk as she made a determined effort to look straight ahead.

She didn't fool anyone in our chapel. They knew when a junkie on the nod was in their midst. Finally she gave up and left, walking with elaborate care. She stayed in her room the rest of the day, and we didn't disturb her. Getting through to her while she was still high would have been impossible, and we didn't waste our time.

Now Eva was dried out, and wary. "I'll try to pull myself into line, Brother Dave," she said. "I'll try real hard, you wait and see!"

"Eva, were you high when you came back on Mon day?" If only she would admit it!

"No!" she said, her eyes wide with pretended horror. "I swear I wasn't! You know I wouldn't do a thing like that!"

A faith that was genuine would have changed Eva. Instead of continuing in a lie she knew wouldn't hold up, she would have admitted her guilt and asked forgiveness. Evidently her faith was little more than the phrases she mouthed so skillfully. "Eva, we're going to dismiss you," I said. She couldn't know how reluctantly I spoke those words.

Eva's face twisted in a grimace of pain, and tears burst from her eyes. She took a deep breath and moaned low in her throat, rocking back and forth, as if she were in agony. "Brother Dave, you can't turn me out!" she sobbed. It was hard to believe she was acting, and I never could have convinced her that she was; she always believed her own lies, and I sometimes wondered if she told them only for herself. "You're a Christian, Brother Dave, you're supposed to help people!" she whimpered. "What are the other girls going to say when you throw me out?"

"Let's get to the truth, Eva," I said. "I can't help you by sitting here, listening to your lies, and patting you on the head as if you were a good girl. You've been

124

warned before, several times, and you still think you can con us! Now, we may be square, but we're not stupid!"

She had no reply. She hung her head, but not in shame; Eva was very angry.

"The other girls know what you've been doing, Eva, and I don't think they'll need any explanation. I'd worry more if we didn't dismiss you. Then we'd have to do a lot of talking."

I wasn't really so sure about the other girls. Eva's prediction was probably more accurate than mine. Chickie and Margarita were still very immature and they would have difficulty understanding any decision we made about Eva's misconduct. Coming back to the Center when she was high was the most serious breach of rules Eva could have committed; it was absolutely demoralizing to our other converts, and I doubted whether any means of discipline could completely restore the damage she had done. She had stimulated old appetites, stirred memories that should have been forgotten. This was the reason we never admitted new people unless they came to us clean; they might be sick, but they had to be clean.

While they would have been hurt by a breakdown in our discipline, the other girls would nevertheless resent us for bringing the rules down on Eva's head. They would sentimentalize, as addicts love to do; they always see themselves as victims, and, sadly, they often are; and while there is much more to the picture, they usually don't see it. Eva's dismissal would be an excuse to go out and get even with the world. As one of our converts had said about her own reason for using drugs,

"I wanted to get back at everybody for hurtin' me, so I'd go out and shoot it up. I figured I might get an O.D.—overdose—accidentally, and then they'd all be sorry I was dead!". Most addicts didn't want to take their own lives, but they often hoped somebody else would.

But Eva would have to leave; and we would soon find out whether our other girls were mature enough to stay.

"Nicky!" I shouted, and jumped up from my chair. Nicky met me halfway across the room, and we shook hands, pumping each other's arm furiously. "Why didn't you let me know you were in town?" I asked.

"I just got here, Dave. Came here first thing!" He grinned. In the years since I had met him, Nicky Cruz had undergone the most startling change I had ever seen. He came to us a tough, violent, hate-driven gang-fighter. He was a minister now, dedicating his life to helping other young boys who were lost in the city streets.

The time seemed to disappear while we talked about his work. Nicky made me feel relaxed and hopeful. I looked at this clear-eyed, neatly dressed, energetic young man, and compared him to the stealthy, arrogant, hostile boy in black leather jacket, tight black jeans, and high black shoes. He was quick with a knife in those days, and deadly, too. Now he carried a Bible and he walked without fear.

The phone rang, and I held up my hand to stop Nicky from speaking. I didn't want to miss a word he had to say. As I picked up the phone, the smile on my lips stiffened.

"I'm gonna kill myself and my kids!" came into my ears. The voice was high and thin, as if the speaker were standing far from the phone at the other end of the line. It was Joan; she was nearly hysterical. Nicky saw the look on my face, and came around to my side of the desk to try to hear what my caller was saying.

"Did you hear me, Mister?" Joan shouted.

"Yes, Joan, I'm here," I said, trying to sound calm.

"I'm not gonna let anybody take my kids!" she said. "I got a knife in my hand right this minute, and I'm gonna kill us all!" She hung up.

Nicky remembered Joan from his days as a street worker in her neighborhood, and he was at my side as I raced out of my office, down the flight of stairs, and into the street. Joan lived two blocks away, and I ran faster than I thought I could. Nicky was only a step behind me when we reached the narrow old building where Joan lived. We were gasping for each breath as we ran up the flight of stairs to the front door, and went into the hall. Joan lived in a front apartment on the first floor, and we threw ourselves against her door, winded and fearful. We hit the door with the flat of our hands and called out to Joan. I almost wept when I heard her voice from inside. She was incoherent and babbling, and the baby was crying.

"What's goin' on here?" I heard behind me. It was the superintendent, a scrawny little man who obviously wasn't frightened by such things as two men trying to break into one of his apartments. He was skeptical when we told him why we were there, but when he listened at Joan's door, he gave in and used his passkey. We rushed past him when the door was opened.

Joan was standing by the bed in the middle of the

room, little Virginia in one arm and a long, ugly kitchen knife in her other hand. There was a strange smile on her face. The baby was unhurt, and Ruth, who was crouched on the bed next to an open suitcase, seemed all right, too. I was looking only for signs of physical harm; I knew both girls had been hurt in ways I couldn't see.

"Put the knife down, Joan," I said, trying to sound matter-of-fact, as if I had just noticed that she had picked it up. She shook her head, smiling slyly, like a child who refused to return something she had snatched from a parent. Before she could lift her arm, I crossed the few steps between us and grasped her wrist. She looked at me in surprise as I pried open her fingers and took the knife from her hand. Nicky took the baby from her.

"I see you're packin', Miss," the superintendent said, contemptuously, nodding toward the suitcase on the bed. "I think that's a good idea. See that you're paid up before you leave." Without another word, he left.

"He's just overcome with sympathy, isn't he?" Nicky said, sarcastically. He picked up a baby's bottle that was on the floor. The milk remaining in it was curdled and flecked with yellow; it must have been there for days.

"I really was gonna do it," Joan said. "If I can't keep my own kids, I'll kill us all!" She sank into a chair and let her head fall back. She wasn't high now, I was quite sure of that, but she had been back on the needle. I saw the ugly little red marks where the needle had entered the veins in her arms. Some of them appeared to be infected.

We couldn't convince Joan that no one was going to take her children away from her without her consent. One of her neighbors had frightened her by calling in the police when Joan didn't come home one night, and a social worker began to call on the children regularly. "They want to send somebody in here to clean up and take care of them," she sneered. "It's a trick. Next thing you know, they'll have me up on charges of abusin' my own children."

"You wouldn't be able to deny those charges, Joan," I said. "You're abusing them now." I put my arm around Ruth's thin shoulders; she was trembling, too shaken to cry. "Do you think they'll forget a scene like this?" Joan shrugged. "Yes, I know what you'll say. 'They can take care of themselves.' I've heard other mothers say the same thing and they think it gets them off the hook. You don't seem to understand that Ruth and Virginia are completely helpless. You might come home from one of your binges and find them dead!"

Joan shook her head. "We'll get along, don't you worry. I won't try anything like this again, I promise." She was brushing us off, and nothing I said could change her mind.

Nicky tried, too. "Give your kids a break, Joan," he said. "Even if you can't make it, maybe they can." She seemed not to hear him. She took Virginia from his arms and laid her on the bed next to little Ruth, whose eyes pleaded with us to stay. I think she was terrified of being left alone with her mother.

I felt so helpless when we left Joan's apartment. We had gone there in such a hurry; now we walked slowly back to the Center, hoping, I suppose, to hear Joan call out to us before we were out of sight. She didn't call. She was probably packing the rest of her family's pitifully few belongings; one scarred, dirty suitcase would hold them all.

Helplessness is the worst defeat I've ever had to take, and I had my fill of it that day. Now I seemed to be back where I started several years ago. I was leaving two little people behind. They needed help, and I wanted to give it to them. Why couldn't I?

"Are you busy, Mom?" She was, but she shook her head and waved me into her office. She spent only part of her day at the Center; our Catacomb Chapel in Greenwich Village was her special project, and she was usually there at night, sitting at a table, ready to talk to beatniks in trouble. Today I needed her special talent for listening, and I had waited for the sound of her voice in her room down the hall from mine.

15

We talked about several unimportant things. Then my mother sat back, folded her arms, and said, "You've got something on your mind, David. I have a feeling it's far more interesting than all this nonsense."

I smiled in appreciation. She had the nicest way of prodding me to get to the point and stop wasting her time. "What would you say if I told you that Teen Challenge was going to make room for the little people?" I asked.

Her expression didn't change. "I'd say, 'Praise the Lord!'—if that's where God is leading you."

"I know it is. I just don't know how to begin. I'll tell you what I have in mind." I began describing something I was beginning to see with my heart.

The little people needed more than homes. They needed families and God. It was no use settling for less than everything they needed to equip them for life in a rough-and-tumble world. I knew of only one door that led to all three of these needs, and that was the door to Teen Challenge. Until now, we seemed to have a revolving door through which our little people came and went; they took our tears with them, but nothing that could really help them.

"Mom, I'm thinking about setting up group homes for the little people, something along the lines of our girls' home, but more closely supervised."

"How large would these homes be?"

"I figure we can take eight to twelve children in each home. We'd have boys and girls of different ages, so they could really feel like a family. We'd have a 'mother' and 'father' at the head of each group, and maybe several staff workers, too. I haven't thought it all out, yet."

"Then it's time you did, David," my mother said, sitting up straight again. Now she was going to bring me down to earth, and that's where I'd have to be if I wanted to start building something. "How much money would these homes cost?" she asked.

"I haven't the slightest idea," I said, reluctant, at that point, to face an ever-present problem. Our needs were already figured down to the penny.

"Well, I certainly can't even guess at the amount, but I'm sure it would be enormous," she said. "That's only one problem," she continued. "You'll have to work your way through miles of red tape where children are concerned. You'll need lawyers, and all kinds of approval by the welfare authorities, and—."

I waved my hand in front of her as if it were a flag of

truce. "Mom, I'll have to take these obstacles one at a time, not all at once!"

She was very businesslike. "You have to realize what's involved in this plan of yours," she said. "You've just described something a little short of heaven for these children, and I'm all for it, but be sure you realize how many obstacles you'll face."

I rested my chin on my clasped hands and stared at the floor. "You know, Mom, God seems to thrive on obstacles," I said. "I remember when Teen Challenge was only an impossible plan, a hope. I don't want to hurt your feelings, Mom, but—."

She was smiling. "David, I'm glad you haven't forgotten that faith, not money, built Teen Challenge. You go ahead and think some more about these children's homes. Pray about them. You've got a good idea." Our talk was finished. She gathered up her mail into a neat stack before her and began to open the letter on top.

Felix and I sat in the chapel. We were the only ones there, and it was a good place to talk. He was very low in spirits.

"This is worse, Dave, not hearing a thing from Doris," he said. "It's been two weeks now."

"Have you passed the word around? Has anyone seen her on their rounds?"

"No one. She just disappeared, and you know a junkie won't go far all by herself." Felix had a genuine love for his wife; it was a gift few addicts were ever offered. What a shame his wife didn't even know it existed!

"When is the baby due, Felix?" I asked.

"Another month, I guess. There's not much time."

We knelt and prayed, not really knowing that the girl in our prayers was still alive. Neither of us had mentioned the possibility that she might be dead, yet that was the most obvious, most frightening answer to Doris' disappearance.

The year was ending in uncertainty for some of our converts. Joan was gone, her two girls with her, and she wasn't the kind to let us know her new address, if she had one. I couldn't escape from an uneasiness I felt when I wondered where she was. Joan had come and gone in moments of crisis; she couldn't survive many more of them.

16

It was New Year's Eve, and I blamed myself for the decision that sent four converts out into the carousing New York streets. I was the one who decided that the holiday was too much of a temptation for young men and women who were trying to forget such things as liquor and drugs. They were only beginning to understand how nightmarish their existence had been; I didn't want them out on the street, running into people who were "having a good time" getting drunk. It didn't make sense.

Most of our converts appreciated our holiday regulation, but some of our girls resented it. They didn't say a word to anyone, not even to each other; they simply exchanged glances, communicating in the wordless way they had known on the street. Then they began to work on the boys. By dinnertime, four young people were missing: Anna and Robert, and Beverly and Pedro.

Usually our converts seem to enjoy being told what

to do, but they do not like to be "bossed." The four runaways had read the wrong meaning into our holiday restrictions and thought we were pushing them around. Because they still didn't respect themselves, they couldn't understand why we were trying to protect them. "I thought they trusted us," Margarita had heard Anna say, "and now they treat us like criminals."

At first we weren't sure that Beverly and Pedro were really missing. They often went out at night, and we suspected that they were drinking again. When they didn't answer our telephone calls, I asked Naomi, one of our staff workers, to stop by their apartment, hoping she wouldn't find Sandra alone. But there she was, alone, lying quietly in her crib, smiling up at Naomi's anxious face.

Again I felt a terrible helplessness coming over me as I thought of little Sandra. "Wouldn't some nice family love to have her!" Naomi had said when she called to tell us that she was going to stay at the apartment. "I just can't believe they've run out on her," she said. "I'm sure they'll come home."

I couldn't quite share her optimism. Beverly and Pedro had been going through the motions of making a home for their baby, but they weren't quite convincing. Their small, dark apartment revealed the very thing I had been feeling about them: so much had been done to cover up its flaws. Plenty of paint had been used on the walls, the cupboards, and almost every piece of furniture. The paint was fresh, bright, and cheerful; the small kitchen table was always set with a gaily printed tablecloth and a vase of pretty paper flowers; bright cushions were tied to the chairs. The whole apartment was immaculately kept, and full of promise, but underneath the decoration it was old and falling apart. Nothing basic had been repaired.

In the refrigerator, Naomi found a bottle of milk, but when she opened it, she didn't like the smell of it. She poured it down the sink. She found a jar of baby food in a cupboard and heated it in a pan on the stove. Then she scraped it into a soup plate—the only plate she could find that wasn't chipped—poked through spoons until she found one that wasn't rough around the edge, and sat down to feed a hungry little girl. Later, when Naomi told me about it, I thought of the children whose food is warmed in special pans or electrical gadgets; they eat from special bowls made and bought just for them, and use special round-edged spoons designed to fit into their tiny mouths without hurting them. Once I may have thought that some of these trappings were foolish; now I had to admit that at least it was a foolishness that came from love.

Another one of our workers volunteered to stay with Sandra later that night. We still couldn't quite believe that Beverly and Pedro had left her as well as us. I stayed in my office, going to the front window every time I thought I heard someone outside. I knew I couldn't sleep, not with four rebellious young people on my mind.

I found a newspaper someone had left behind and looked through it. I hadn't the patience to read it. Suddenly I turned back to a page I had just passed. I don't know why the small headline caught my attention; it mentioned no names. It read very simply: WOMAN, TWO

GIRLS, KILLED IN FIRE. The story was short: A woman, apparently under the influence of drugs or liquor, had fallen unconscious in her tenement apartment; a cigarette was left burning, and a fire started, trapping two little girls with their mother. The victims' identities were not yet determined, but the apartment had been rented to a woman named Joan Carpenter.

Joan, Ruth and Virginia, all of them gone! Joan and her habit had a death grip on each other, and the violence of their struggle had finally destroyed two innocent children. What a terrible place the world must have seemed to Ruth and Virginia! Love and friendship always had to keep their legal distance, but fear, loneliness, anger, and finally death were intimate companions. Again, I went back over the last time I had seen the girls alive, and came to the same unhappy conclusion: there had been no way to help them.

My eyes were heavy with fatigue, but I wanted to wait until morning before acknowledging that Beverly and Pedro weren't coming back. "What will happen to Sandra if they don't?" I asked myself aloud, and I shook my head. I didn't have an answer. It didn't seem possible that this child, too, would soon be lost.

A prayer came from somewhere deep inside me. "I don't know what to do with her, God. You must have had some reason for bringing her to us. Jesus told us how You felt about the little people, and I know You want us to help them. But how? Where can we take them? Where do they belong?"

Don called me early the next morning. Beverly had just come home; she was alone. When I arrived at the apartment, she was in tears. "He stole my record player!" she wailed. "That fink took my record player!" She dropped into a corner of the sofa and slammed her fist into the cushion.

17

Don nodded sadly toward the bedroom where Sandra slept. "She doesn't seem to be worried about her," he said.

Beverly was a beautiful girl, even when her face was swollen with tears. She was very small and delicate, and it was hard to look at her and believe that she was anything but innocent.

"Where's Pedro?" I asked. She sobbed and shook her head. "Why didn't he come home with you?"

Beverly sighed. "I thought he was here all night. That's why I didn't worry about Sandra. I didn't know she was alone," she said. She held up her clenched fists. "That rat! He told me he was going home to watch the baby! He must have come in here before you came— and he stole my record player!" She pointed to an empty end table where, I assumed, the record player must have rested. "That was the most precious thing in the world to me! He *knew* that!"

The record player came first, and who knows where

Sandra stood in the line of Beverly's affections. I was sickened by what I heard. "Is Pedro back on the needle?" I asked.

"You bet he is! He's been back on it for two weeks. Don't you notice how many things are missing around here? You can find them at the nearest hock shop if you want them back, but you'll have to shell out the dough for them!" There were no more tears now; in fact, she seemed to take pleasure in telling us about her husband. "He's no good," she said. "Don't waste your time on him."

Was she right, and did her advice apply to her as well? Were we wasting our time, and God's as well, by trying to bring these twisted young people to a realization that they could live useful lives? It wasn't enough for us to want something better for them; *they* had to want it, too. For Beverly and Pedro, that meant a complete transformation had to take place somewhere deep inside them. Instead of playing games with us, they had to be able to look at the ugliness of their lives and see it for the mess it was.

I knew what we were up against when we worked with the street people. I didn't expect results overnight. Still, I used to have much more patience. I knew better than to take Beverly's advice; her angry words were a slum kid's way of calling for help; the cry was feeble and distant, but I could nevertheless hear it. She was testing me, and in his more drastic way, Pedro was doing the same thing.

It was the little people who were making me impatient with some of the big people. They turned each second into a matter of extreme urgency. I had been trying to divide my heart between them and their parents, and so I was being torn in two.

"Sleep it off, Beverly," I said. "We'll take Sandra to the Bentons' house while you get some rest. You need it." She looked at me suspiciously; she couldn't believe that I meant what I said. "You're not going to throw us out?" she asked, and in her childlike anxiety she looked as young as Sandra.

"No, Beverly. Get some rest now." We bundled Sandra in a few blankets and took her with us. She had slept through it all.

John Benton had his share of trouble, too. From his home across the street from the Center, he happened to see Anna and Robert slip into their apartment early that morning, and as he was on his way to talk to them he heard the sound of breaking glass. Looking up in the direction of the noise, he saw a chair leg protruding from a broken window on the second floor, where Anna and Robert lived. Inside, he heard curses and angry shouts coming from upstairs, and he ran into Robert halfway up the stairs. Blood came from a cut in the boy's temple; he mumbled something John couldn't understand until he saw Anna standing at the top of the stairs with a heavy lamp base in her hand. The right side of her face was puffy and red, and her lip was bleeding. She and Robert had been swinging at each other with razor blades, as well as furniture. They were high, but not on heroin alone; they had gorged themselves on goofballs, too, and that was the reason for the violence.

Most addicts are cautious about taking "goofballs,"

which is a slang term for a powerful barbiturate. It is sold in the form of a pill, and can be taken orally, which means the addict doesn't have to worry about someone finding his works (the crude equipment used to prepare and inject heroin); it can be thrown away quickly, in case the police are suspicious. It is also tricky and unreliable, as far as its effects are concerned. Heroin dulls a user, and the better the "stuff," the duller the user. Goofballs are entirely different; an addict never knows how he'll react when he takes them, but he can be sure he'll move around a lot. He might even get pretty mean if he doesn't like the way someone looks at him. Goofballs are dangerous, not only to the addict, but to anybody within his reach.

When Anna and Robert left us on New Year's Eve, they went out looking for a connection because they wanted to get even with us for the hurt they imagined we had caused them to suffer. Not many blocks from the Center they had run into an old acquaintance, a woman who used to "cop" for them, and she agreed to do them the same old favor. She took every cent they had on them (it was only five dollars) and promised to come back in fifteen minutes with a bag of heroin— "nothing but the good stuff." It was an old game, and Anna and Robert knew they were taking a risk by trusting another addict with the money to buy a fix; she might spend it on her own habit. But they were in a reckless mood, and they couldn't believe that any addict would be so low as to steal a fix from friends who hadn't had one in months. They were wrong. They had been among new friends for so long that they forgot what friendship meant out on the street. The woman never came back, and Anna and Robert had to duck under the subway turnstiles to sneak a ride into Manhattan, where they borrowed money from their relatives. They did their own copping then, and they bought everything the pushers were selling—heroin, marijuana, pep pills, goofballs—to make up for lost time. They got even, all right, but somehow it wasn't very satisfying.

John and some of the staff members kept Anna and Robert apart until their high wore off. Anna was the first to come back to her senses, and she was almost weak with remorse and shame. She tried to fuss over Robert and begged his forgiveness when she saw the cut on his head. "How could I do such a thing?" she cried. "I must have been crazy!" John led her into the chapel, and there she stayed for the rest of the day. She knelt most of the time, and when I looked in on her later, I saw that some of our staff were kneeling by her side, praying with her.

"I thought I was safe," she told us later. "I thought I'd never want another fix as long as I lived. What a dope I was!" Anna and Robert had behaved like children, and they were the first to admit it. "We should have known you were trying to help us when you told us to stay here," Robert said. "But no, just like kids, we had to go out and prove that you couldn't tell us what to do!" In talking about himself, Robert was describing all the other big people out on the street. They all were children, no matter how many years they had lived in the world; and they wanted all the love, care, and attention they had missed by not having had a childhood.

143

In a way, they were refusing to grow up until they got what was owed them; yet it was a debt the world could never repay. So there the big people stayed, between infancy and adulthood, and there they would stagnate unless they were rescued by a love greater than any they had been denied. God's love, once it got into the human heart, had a way of maturing an infantile spirit; I had seen it happen often. The difficulty lay in unlocking the human heart; it had to be done from the inside.

The little people didn't stand a chance unless the big people grew up. Anna's fears for her coming child made this painfully clear. "How can I take care of a baby?" she asked. "*I* behave like a baby!" At last she had stopped telling herself fairy tales about motherhood; she was awakening to its responsibilities, and she had good reason to doubt the way she would handle them. Yet, Anna's reaction was, in itself, encouraging. Unlike Eva, who could not look at her life honestly, Anna knew she had done wrong by leaving the Center. Going back to a drug-drowsy world hadn't been the kick she and her husband had sought. "It's different when you know there's a right and a wrong way to live," Anna said. "It just isn't fun to be wrong any more." What she meant was that she was beginning to face the truth about her past. She could no longer lie about it, not even to herself. Now she was ready to look into her future with honesty; she would be able to see the pitfalls, the temptations, the burdens, and demands that lie in everyone's path, and, seeing them, she would begin to understand how she could make her way through them without falling down. She was not alone. She had a Saviour who would take her by the hand.

144

"Doris got busted!" Felix shouted over the telephone, making my ear ring. I couldn't understand why he was so happy about his wife being in jail.

18

"When?" I asked, sleepily; the telephone had awakened me.

"A couple of weeks ago," he said. "That's why I didn't hear from her. She got caught breaking into a store."

"Well, what's good about that?" I snapped.

"I'm gettin' to it, Dave, just give me time!" Felix was out of breath. "She had the baby, Dave! A girl!" he said.

"Wonderful, Felix! How are they? And where are they?"

"Man, they're great! They're in the prison maternity ward." Felix became serious. "Dave, Doris wants to come here when they let her out. She got a short sentence, and now that the baby's here, she thinks they'll suspend the rest of it, especially if she has a place to live." He hesitated. "How about it? You got room for my family here?"

Felix had once told me that "Christianity is a way-out thing." He meant it as a compliment. "You gotta be tough to live that way," he said, and that's exactly what he had proved himself to be. He was young in faith; he wasn't entirely convinced that God was looking out for

145

him, and it had taken courage to live up to his own doubts. Doris hadn't made it easier for him.

"I think we can fix up an apartment for you," I said, "if Doris means what she says."

"I wish you could talk to her, Dave. I couldn't believe it was my own wife talkin' to me. Somethin' changed her."

"You've given me an idea, Felix," I said. "I'll drop in and see her at the prison ward tomorrow." He was silent, and I realized that I had forgotten something; Felix hadn't seen his baby girl yet. "Want to come along?" I asked.

"I sure do!" he shouted. My guess was right; he was reluctant to go alone.

Every now and then we have a truly blessed day at the Center, a day that seems to make up for all the disappointments we've known. Felix had awakened me to such a day.

I went over to the girls' home to have breakfast with the Bentons, and John told me that he had met Eva during his rounds the past night. "You know what she said, Dave?" I shook my head. "She said, 'It ain't the same as it used to be. I know better now, and I'm uncomfortable living like this.'"

It was happening. Sometimes we were too easily disappointed. Sometimes we forgot that God is the One with endless patience; we human beings tire of waiting, and we begin to think we may have set our dreams too high. Now I saw that I was not only impatient, but quite wrong. Some of the big people simply couldn't give up their past all at once. They kept feeling the call

146

to go back and see the old friends, the old places; and often they had to wallow in the old sins once more to find out if they were really as bad as they remembered them to be. They were taking a risk, and they usually got hurt, but not all of them had to end their lives as Jennie did. Some of them might find, as Eva and Anna and Robert did, that they had already been amazingly changed by their grudging acceptance of God's love. A bit of maturity had come to them, and with it some small degree of self-respect; kicks now seemed degrading.

I remembered something Eva had told me long ago, when she first began to behave herself during chapel services. "I don't like people with vices," she said, and I was surprised at the clarity of her mind once she was off drugs. "I know I'm not one of them, but I've always admired people who were cool—you know, the kind who could take care of their problems without the help of a bottle or a bag of H. Someday I'd like to be one of those people." Perhaps she would, someday.

"Does she want to come back?" I asked John.

"Indeed she does!" he said, with a happy grin. "And I think she will. But I don't want to say 'yes' right away. I don't want her to think she can duck in and out of here. Coming back has to mean something to her."

One by one, the members of our Center family were coming back. Even though it was a new and demanding experience, family living had begun to mean something to our girls. It was love put to everyday use.

Each day was bringing more answers to our prayers. Neither John nor I mentioned it, but I think we were hoping for the same thing: one of these days, we might be hearing from Shirley, too.

Doris was thankful for the time she spent in jail. As she said, it probably saved her baby's life. As I listened to her, I had to agree with Felix: she wasn't the same young woman.

19

At first, when Doris was caught and arrested for stealing, she blamed God, as she always did when something unpleasant happened to her. And when the judge was unmoved by her tears, and sentenced her to jail, Doris was sure that God was out to get her. Like many other big people, she thought of God in human terms, comparing Him with the people she had known; if she had treated her junkie friends as she had treated God, she would have made some enemies.

Doris decided to pay God back by doing the one thing she had refused to do while she was at Teen Challenge. She would give her life over to Him. The laugh would be on God, because the life she was ready to turn over to His keeping was a real booby prize. "Okay, Jesus, I'm all yours!" she had snarled in her cell. She had the strangest feeling that she was not alone; Someone seemed to be there, listening.

Another strange thing happened during her first few days in jail; she felt a change come over her. She had begun to talk to Jesus, strictly as a joke, but she was beginning to depend upon these conversations. They

149

made her feel less lonely, less guilty and frightened; even her most confusing thoughts began to untangle themselves.

"I don't know why, but I asked the guard for a Bible one day," Doris said. "I guess she figured I was a psycho or something, but she brought one, anyway. I began to read it, straight through from the beginning. I always wanted to do somethin' like that, y'know?"

Doris found that she was no longer joking; she had truly given her life to God. "I caught myself thinkin' about Him instead of dope, and my days weren't empty anymore. There was so much love in my heart that I thought the seams were bustin'."

Because Doris was in jail and away from her supply of narcotics during the few weeks before the birth of her baby, her little girl was spared a horrible experience. "The girl in the next bed had a baby at the same time, only she was still hooked when she checked into the hospital. You should see what her kid went through!" Doris was not exaggerating. Fifty to eighty percent of the babies born to addicted mothers are addicted, too. Shortly after they come into the world, they have to fight their way through withdrawal, and in their weakened newborn state, not many of them make it.

I promised Doris that we would look for a foster family to care for her baby until she and Felix were ready to make a home for her. Doris was eager to come back to Teen Challenge, and she seemed rather proud that her husband had had the strength to stay there.

There was a time when addicted newborn babies were cases for the medical books. Now there are many of them, enough to attract the attention of the newspapers.

It is hard to imagine anything more pitiful than the world's littlest addicts. They are born to mothers who cannot kick their drug habit for even a few days, the minimum time required to guarantee the "clean" birth of an addict's baby. Some hospitals have set up prenatal programs for addicted mothers in the hope that they can persuade and help them to make this small sacrifice, but the record of their success is not encouraging. Most pregnant addicts do what Doris would have done is she hadn't been in jail: they stay away from the hospital until the very last minute, and then they take a final fix before checking in. If the doctors discover that a mother is an addict, they will usually treat her newborn infant for withdrawal; at the very least, they will keep very close watch over the baby in case withdrawal symptoms should appear. In such cases, a hospital has the right to detain the infant for treatment, even over the mother's protests.

A junkie mother tries to keep her habit a secret because she doesn't want anybody telling her she ought to give it up for the baby's sake. She knows what she's done, and she wants to keep running away from it, so she spends as little time as possible in a hospital. Legally, she has the right to leave, taking her baby with her, as soon after birth as she can walk, and many addicted mothers stay no longer than twenty-four hours after they check in. Physically, this is risky for the mother, but for the child, it is almost surely fatal.

The problem for the newborn addict is not one of getting enough drugs for his habit, but of trying to survive the loss of his supply. He has been fed through his mother's bloodstream, and the act of birth cuts him off from his lethal food. No longer nourished—and drugged—by his mother, the baby begins to go through cold turkey. For a tiny, fragile infant, this is more than a severe discomfort; it is a terrible ordeal of vomiting, diarrhea, and excruciating pain, and if the baby is not treated immediately, he will die from the loss of his body fluids and the consequent collapse of his blood vessels.

As long as they are in a hospital and known to be addicted, these "withdrawal babies" can be cured; in fact, they are the only addicts in the world who can be cured strictly by medical means—they have not lived long enough to become emotionally hooked. Their greatest need at this critical time is constant care, and this is the last thing they will ever get if they are sent home with their addicted mothers. Homecoming, in their cases, means almost certain death. Even if they have been successfully treated in a hospital, these little babies need special care and attention during their first few weeks at home, and they aren't likely to get it. A junkie mother is a bad nurse; she thinks *she* has problems!

Heroin, in its purer forms, used to act as a contraceptive, and a woman who was able to satisfy her habit simply didn't get pregnant. In that way, the agony of the drug world was restricted to one generation at a time. But narcotics is now a big business, and its stockholders are ravenous for profits; not content with their growing numbers of customers, they are diluting the merchandise to the point where some addicts are shooting nothing but quinine or milk sugar into their veins.

Unfortunately, the poor quality of the product isn't driving away the customers. Narcotics is a filthy business, and its customers expect to be cheated; dilution simply means that addicts have to move up to a bigger habit to get any kick at all, which in turn means that they have to get their hands on more money. Junkies have their rat race, too, and the women get the worst of it.

An addicted woman hates to open her eyes and face the day. She needs a shot to calm her nerves, because the sight of life, first thing in the morning, shakes her up. If she had been a cool one the night before, she tucked a fix away somewhere; if she'd been greedy, as most addicts are, she was in trouble. Prostitution isn't the kind of business that can be carried on during daylight hours, and if she had to go all day without a fix, she'd be too sick to work at night; she had to be just right—between coming down from a high and going into withdrawl—to make a living.

With a fix, a woman can make it through a few hours, and she isn't going to worry about buying the next fix until she needs it. Without a fix, she begins to get frantic. She tries to squeeze a few dollars out of her neighbors, her relatives, her friends, but she's been through this before, and everyone is wise to her. No one will listen to her wild stories, and so she goes out on the street to see what she can steal. All this time, she has a boyfriend waiting for his fix, too. It's a rough life, but once they both get their hands on some "stuff" and settle back into a nice high, they forget how horrible it really is.

Now the highs are harder to come by, no matter how many fixes a junkie gets. A girl has to work twice as hard to get the stuff, and it isn't taking her off the ground any more. As if things weren't bad enough, she has to worry about getting pregnant; she sees it happening to lots of her friends.

It was true; so many more babies had been born to addicted mothers during the past few years, and most of them suffered from withdrawal. The newborn-baby addict, once a rarity in the medical world, was becoming a tragic concern for all mankind. Teen Challenge was already involved in it.

I was beginning to see things differently. Our problem was not that of reaching the little people, but of holding onto them. From the pitifully weakened babies in a hospital nursery to restless youngsters like Jose and Margarita, the danger was the same. Would they stay in one place long enough to be treated? The addicted babies needed medical attention; Jose and Margarita needed spiritual care. Would they live long enough to get it? And if they did survive, would they grow up in a world of junkies?

Unwelcome in the world, exposed to its cruelties, and unprotected from its violence, what chance did the little people have to survive their so-called "childhood"? I had known three of those who died; I feared for the lives of thousands more. Holding onto these children, once they came our way, was now a matter of life and death.

I was tired of knocking on other doors. I had to find a way to open our own door to the little people. It had to be done immediately, before another child walked out of my sight and became lost.

As my mother had said, the group homes were a great idea, but making them come to life seemed impossible. Perhaps that's why I knew this plan was right for us.

Teen Challenge had been another one of those "impossible" ideas only a few years ago. Even I thought I was out of my mind to leave a pleasant country parsonage and come to New York to tell gang-fighters about the Christ who could save them. Now I was thankful that God doesn't always work in rational ways.

I had work to do, and I began it in our chapel. I found Anna and Robert praying there, and I knelt beside them. "Dear Lord," I prayed, "these two young people will soon become parents, and they're scared stiff. So am I, Lord, because I've seen what happens to the little people, and I don't want their baby to be one of them.

"Now, we're open to anything you want us to do for this baby, but so far our best idea is a home, a real home, where he or she can live until Anna and Robert are ready to take over. This may take a long time, God, because Anna and Robert can't even take over their own lives yet. They may even fall on their faces a few more times.

"We'd like to take care of this baby, God, and we'd like to make sure that he or she gets to know You. It won't be enough to give this baby a good home, and some wonderful substitute parents; we think this child ought to get to know Jesus as a Friend. This baby will have a special need for His kind of love; then, no matter what might happen to him later in his life, he'll never feel abandoned or unloved or worthless. He'll never want to hurt other people, because he'll know how much You love them, too. And he'll never have contempt for his own life, because he'll realize how much it means to You.

156

"This is a big order, Lord, because we want to hold onto as many little people as we can find. It's Teen Challenge all over again, and You know what that means. It seems impossible; it'll take a long time; and it'll cost a lot of money. And yet I feel that this is the way You want us to go."

I dug in my pocket and pulled out a crumpled letter. "I got this in the mail this morning, Lord. It's from Chickie. She's been preaching at some churches near her Bible school, and taking a collection after she preaches. She sent us eighty-two dollars she collected, and told us to use it for Your work. I'm going to use it to open an account for our children's homes, and pray hard for the rest."

The rest would come; I was certain of that. Very soon, the little people would be in our midst. Only then would I have peace.

From the days of Dave Wilkerson's first encounter with young toughs on city streets, so dramatically recounted in THE CROSS AND THE SWITCHBLADE, Dave and his staff have seen the changing face of need and responded to its call. TWELVE ANGELS FROM HELL introduced the world to the desperate struggle of the dope addict and what *Teen Challenge* is doing to salvage broken lives. Now you've met "The Little People" —helpless, hopeless victims of big people's sin —whose haunting cries can no longer be ignored.

If you wish to share in Reverend Wilkerson's work, his address is:

TEEN CHALLENGE
444 Clinton Avenue
Brooklyn, New York 11238